THE KINGDOM CODE™

MAKE AND MANAGE MONEY... GOD'S WAY!

EMPOWERING STUDENTS TO BE ENTREPRENEURS

BUILD A BUSINESS

DEVELOP CHARACTER

PREPARE FOR THE FUTURE

JOEYS Educational Systems, Inc.
PO Box 422
Dublin, Texas 76446
www.TheKingdomCode.com

Acknowledgments

While attending a Christian conference, the question was asked, "What can you do for the Kingdom of God?" I instantly knew what God wanted me to do. I was to equip students *at an early age* with money management skills based upon Biblical principals. As the writing of **The Kingdom Code** progressed, it became even more evident why God had blessed me with a wonderful family, successful businesses, classroom teaching experiences, and valuable life lessons. My entire life, He had been guiding and preparing me to share this knowledge with the next generation.

I felt students needed the hands-on experience of growing businesses of their very own. That way, they would understand, first-hand, the joys and challenges that come with entrepreneurship. They needed financial skills, social and life lessons, organizational skills, letters of encouragement, and a Biblically-based value system... ***all rolled into one fun and exciting course***... and I was supposed to make it happen!

With the help of God, many gifted people, much prayer, and a lot of perseverance, **The Kingdom Code** is ready to guide students on the pathway to *Make and Manage Money... God's Way*!

I am eternally grateful to everyone who made this curriculum possible. I especially thank Louanne Marshall and Jennifer Hilder, whose help was monumental. Louanne, a home-school mom of seven children, spent countless hours editing, advising, writing, and meticulously correcting the manuscript. Louanne was invaluable. Jennifer Hilder, with experience in teaching at home, a private Christian school, and public school, added a wealth of creative, fun, and insightful material relevant to today's students, teachers, and educational requirements. Richard Toland breathed life into the lessons by carefully weaving the text with pictures and graphics.

Throughout the process, family and friends were my backbone of support. My husband kept me focused, and took over many of my duties. I am grateful to my two children and their spouses, Kate and Bryan, and John and Kristi, who offered great ideas, while giving moral support. From the bottom of my heart comes a huge *thank you* to my grandchildren: Brennan, Caden, John, Graham, and MaKenzie. My sister, Billie, uplifted me. My mentor, Marj Carpenter, had faith in me. My friends Karen Williams, Colleen Harris, Kathy Sherrod, Merlene Byler, and Luanne Schexnider encouraged me. Most importantly, I give tribute to my parents, Kate and Sid Hall. They taught me to put God first, work hard, love others, and live life to the fullest.

Jimmie Byler
Author

Chief Editor
Louanne Marshall

Contributing Editors
Jennifer Hilder
Kate Forsythe

Writing Contributors
Louanne Marshall
Jennifer Hilder
Dallas Marshall

Chief Production Team
Richard Toland
Anna Kalinichenko

Production Team
Joshua Cervantes
Diana Cervantes
Kimberli Burns
Brian Mays
Joanna Friebele
Ashley McLean

Editing Team
Toni Swayze
Billie Earle
Kristen Bolander

Contributing Designers
Aoife Kelly
David Munoz
Christine Mansueto
Robert Cantu
Andrea Bartula

Kingdom Code Kids are Great Leaders and Entrepreneurs. We...

- Follow the **KCK Sales Code**.

- Trust God to guide us.

- Know what is happening in our businesses.

- Work hard to be the best at what we do.

- Manage our money well.

- Treat others like we want to be treated.

KCKs choose to be outstanding Knights in God's Army!

KCKs

Army of God

iv

Table of Contents

Lesson 1

Path to The Kingdom Code

Would you like to start your very own business? Earn money? Learn how to save money to buy things you want? This textbook, **The Kingdom Code**, will show you how to do it. So, what is **The Kingdom Code**?

The Kingdom Code is the pathway to make and manage money God's way.

God rules His Kingdom with love and created you to do great things in His Kingdom. He gave you a code, or a set of rules, to help you make good decisions. If you follow **The Kingdom Code**, it will take you on a journey of adventure and bravery that will last a lifetime!

To discover the keys of how to manage your money and set up a business, you will learn the subject of **economics** (ek-uh-**nom**-iks). Economics is the study of people using their time, talents, and money to produce, buy, and sell goods and services.

In **The Kingdom Code**, you will also learn how to build **Treasure** and find **Clues** to guide you. Every time you open this book, you become a Kingdom Code Kid, or a **KCK**. A **KCK** is a mighty knight in God's army. Today is your first day of many new adventures. Let's get started!

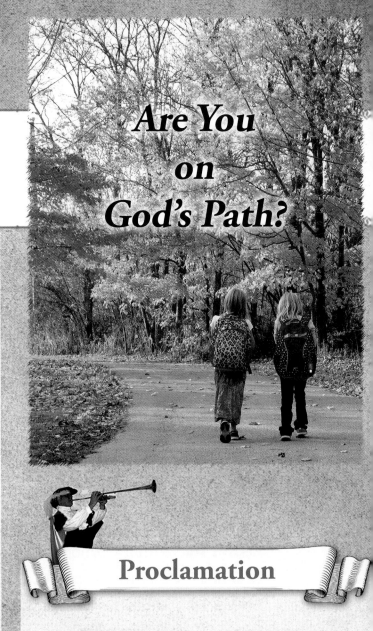

Are You on God's Path?

Proclamation

A **proclamation** (prok-luh-**mā**-shun) is an important statement said out loud.

Every lesson begins with a **Proclamation** that will help you become brave and build faith! Let's look at the first *Proclamation*.

I trust in the Lord with all my heart and depend on Him instead of myself. In everything I do, I honor and remember Him, and He makes my path straight.

After you read the *Proclamation*, always take a moment to think about what it means to you. Then, as a **KCK**, stand and say it out loud.

Check Your Path

In **Check Your Path**, you will use a Worksheet to answer questions about the lesson. A green flag will be your reminder.

 Remove, and let's begin *Worksheet 1: Path to The Kingdom Code* (behind *Worksheets* tab in your **KCK Binder**).

Quest for the Clue

A quest is a journey to search for something. In **Quest for the Clue**, you will search for clues to learn about **The Kingdom Code**.

In each lesson, your quest is to find the **Clue to the Code**. The **Clue** helps you understand how God wants you to live and manage your money. Let's look for the first **Clue to the Code**.

The Bible tells about something special you are to *put on* every day for protection. As you read the verses, try to find what it is, and you will discover the **Clue**.

Finally, be strong in the Lord and in his mighty power. Put on the full armor of God, so that you can take your stand against the devil's schemes.

...Stand firm then, with the belt of truth buckled around your waist, with the breastplate of righteousness in place, and with your feet fitted with the readiness that comes from the gospel of peace.

In addition to all this, take up the shield of faith, with which you can extinguish all the flaming arrows of the evil one. Take the helmet of salvation and the sword of the Spirit, which is the word of God.

— Ephesians 6:10-11, 14-17 NIV

As a **KCK**, you just found the first **Clue to the Code**.

🔍 **All Knights need to put on the full Armor of God for protection.**

If you are wearing the Armor of God, you are ready to fight anything that tries to keep you from being a leader in God's army!

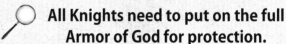

Your teacher will now give you instructions for putting on the full Armor of God. Please stand as your teacher reads. Pretend you are putting on the armor.

I Put On...

THE **BREASTPLATE** OF **RIGHTEOUSNESS**

THE **BELT** OF **TRUTH**

THE **SWORD** OF THE **SPIRIT**

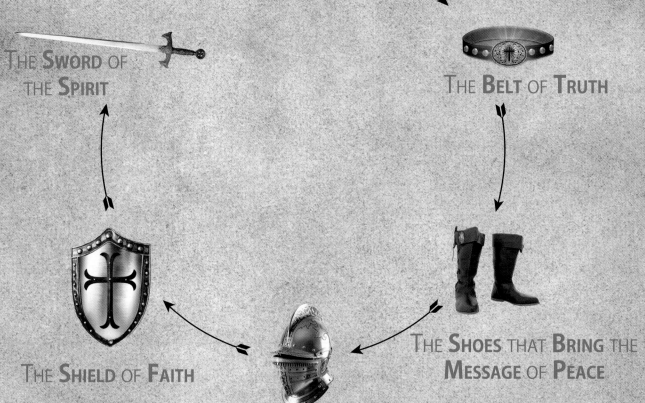

THE **SHOES** THAT **BRING** THE **MESSAGE** OF **PEACE**

THE **SHIELD** OF **FAITH**

THE **HELMET** OF **SALVATION**

Kingdom Code Kids Think Differently!

Wearing the Armor of God, we have God's mighty power to help us.

Code of Honor

In every lesson, the **Code of Honor** has a Bible verse and a Character (**kair**-ik-ter) Code that describes the way a **KCK** thinks and acts. Look at the Character Code on the shield below. Do you know what it means to be...

financially responsible
(fi-**nan**-shuh-lē) (rē-**spon**-suh-buhl)

Financially responsible means spending money wisely, paying what you owe, and not spending more than you can afford.

Be Financially Responsible

What does the Bible say about being financially responsible?

Give to everyone what you owe them. Do you owe taxes? Then pay them. Do you owe anything else to the government? Then pay it. Do you owe respect? Then give it. Do you owe honor? Then show it. Pay everything you owe...
— Romans 13:7-8a NIRV

God's Word tells you to pay every **debt** (det). Debt is money you owe. When you pay all your debts, you are the financially responsible person God wants you to be. He is proud of you, and it is **The Kingdom Code** way.

Being financially responsible is one of the many keys to **The Kingdom Code**. You must choose to put the key in the lock and follow His Word. This means you pay every...

financial responsibility
(fi-**nan**-shul) (rē-spon-suh-**bil**-i-tē)

A **financial responsibility is** a debt or a bill.

KCKs, always pay your debts or bills quickly. For example, if you leave your wallet at home and borrow money from your brother, pay him back as soon as you get home.

Knowing the difference between having a *financial responsibility* and being *financially responsible* is very important.

A financial responsibility is a debt. When you pay a debt, you are being financially responsible.

FINANCIAL RESPONSIBILITY

FINANCIALLY RESPONSIBLE

Say the words above out loud. Do you hear the difference?

Treasure Seeking

There are many treasures in God's Kingdom. In **Treasure Seeking,** you will discover facts that lead you to the **Treasures of the Kingdom**. With God's help, the **Treasures** will help you start and build a business to make money.

Knights, in **The Kingdom Code**, a business is called a...

Why would a business be called a *Treasure Builder*?

If you work and make money in a business, you **build treasure**. The money you earn is called **income** (**in**-kum). Income is money received.

⚜ Share Your Thoughts ⚜

Discuss the following questions to understand the difference between these two ideas.

1. How can you have a financial responsibility and **not** be a financially responsible person?

2. Name some debts or bills your family has to pay every month. An example would be a water bill.

   Each debt is a *financial responsibility*!

3. Talk about something you bought in the past and used your own money to pay for it.

   You were *financially responsible*!

For your first Treasure Builder, you will choose a service business. It is called a *service business* because you will be paid to do a service for others. Examples would be babysitting or washing windows.

❖– Action Time –❖

Let's play a game about different ways to earn income.

1. In your **KCK Binder**, find the *Treasure Builder Ideas* (behind *Forms/Notices* tab). Look at the Service Businesses, and choose some jobs you like.

2. Act out the service jobs for your teacher or classmates. See if they can guess what you are doing.

3. Trade places. Can you guess what others are doing?

Work can be Fun!

As you make money in your first business, you will save your income in a special, zippered pocket. It will be fun to see how much money you earn from your first Treasure Builder.

On your mark!

Get set!

Charge!

🎺 Look again at all the businesses listed in *Treasure Builder Ideas*. Choose five service businesses that sound fun to you. Then, write them on #9 of *Worksheet 1*.

On your great adventure as a **KCK**, you are about to create your own Treasure Builder. It will be exciting and fun to build this business and watch it grow!

Knights, you have just found the first **Treasure of the Kingdom**.

Every KCK will own a Treasure Builder.

Kingdom Code Kids are Part of God's Army!

KCKs, you belong to this mighty army and will make, save, and spend money God's way as you build your first Treasure Builder. In God's army, you will work, help others, and become financially responsible. That is **The Kingdom Code** way!

On Your Own

These are activities you can complete in class or at home.

1. Complete *Activity 1: A Knight's Quest.* When complete, file *Activity 1: A Knight's Quest* in your **KCK Binder** behind *Treasure Builder 1* tab. Show someone your painted rock.

2. Practice counting money with another person. One person names an amount, such as $4.28. The other person counts back the money. (*You can make your own play money.*)

Kingdom Keys

Kingdom Keys are a review of the lesson. Learn all the Key Terms that are bold and in color. Many of the Key Terms are words used in business.

Key to the Lesson
In God's armor, I will be financially responsible and build treasure!

Key Ideas

Clue to the Code
All Knights need to put on the full Armor of God for protection.

Character Code
Be Financially Responsible

Treasure of the Kingdom
Every **KCK** will own a Treasure Builder.

Key Terms

debt (det) money you owe

economics (ek-uh-**nom**-iks) the study of people using their time, talents, and money to produce, buy, and sell goods and services

financial responsibility (fi-**nan**-shul) (rē-spon-suh-**bil**-i-tē) a debt or a bill

financially responsible (fi-**nan**-shuh-lē) (rē-**spon**-suh-bul) spending money wisely, paying what you owe, not spending more than you can afford

income (**in**-kum) money received

proclamation (prok-luh-**mā**-shun) an important statement said out loud

Complete *Worksheet 1: Path to The Kingdom Code*.
File behind *Treasure Builder 1* tab in your KCK Binder.

After you understand and complete each lesson, you can advance one level on the KCK Treasure Map. Each reward brings you a step closer to finding God's treasures!

CONGRATULATIONS

You may place your Level One reward on the KCK Treasure Map!

Bonus Code Work

Earn bonus rewards by completing activities in Bonus Code Work.

1. Draw or use building blocks or clay to make a person who has on the Armor of God. Think about what each piece means. You may label each one. Make it special!

2. Tell someone or write the story of how you chose Christ as your Savior. Try to include how old you were, where you were, who was with you, and how it made you feel. If you were baptized, tell about it.

3. Look at businesses where you live. Make an economics chart. List five or more examples in each column. Number 1 is done for you.

Examples of Economics	
Businesses That Sell Goods	Businesses that Sell Services
1. Tom's Shoes	1. Tom's Shoe Repair
2. ?	2. ?
3. ?	3. ?

4. With your parent's permission, use the internet to search for "money games for kids". Play some online money games for fun.

5. Learn the words to the song on the next page. You can make up hand motions.

Kingdom Code Kids Think Differently!

Chorus
Kingdom Code Kids think differently
Living our lives with integrity.
I'll make and manage money God's way.
I'm a Kingdom Code Kid!

Verse
I want to learn what I can do
To make good choices today,
'Cause I want to be the kind of kid
That follows **The Kingdom Code** way.

Chorus

Verse
So come with me if you want to learn
How to follow **The Kingdom Code** path.
We'll set our goals to find success
Building treasure that lasts.

Chorus

Lesson 2

Prepare to Build Treasure

Proclamation

I choose to work!

Knights, choosing to work is a choice most people have. If you find a job you love, it can be awesome. Work is fun when you enjoy what you do.

In this lesson, you will learn about someone who chose to work. He made a huge impact on the whole world. **KCKs**, it may be God's plan for you to make a difference in the world too.

Take a few moments to think about what the *Proclamation* means to you. Now, stand and repeat the *Proclamation*. While standing, put on the whole Armor of God.

Check Your Path

W Begin *Worksheet 2: Prepare to Build Treasure.*

Quest for the Clue

Long ago, a farmer walked slowly behind a horse and guided a plow to make long furrows (**fur**-ōz). It was not easy and took a long time to get a field ready for planting seeds.

Can you imagine how hard it was when the dirt was thick and sticky? Many times, the farmer would have to stop and clean the heavy mud from his iron plow.

Then, in 1837, one man changed history! He used a leftover piece of steel to invent a polished-steel plow. It slid easily through the mud and hard ground. This man was a true **entrepreneur** (ahn-truh-pruh-**noor**). An entrepreneur is a person who takes a risk to start and manage a business. His name was John Deere.

Many other types of farming equipment were manufactured (man-yuh-**fak**-cherd) by Mr. Deere during his life.

These many inventions (in-**ven**-shunz) made the farmers' work easier and faster. Today, you can repair, service, and buy many types of farming and heavy equipment at John Deere stores all over the world.

This great business was started with an idea, a leftover piece of steel, and a lot of hard work. In his lifetime, John Deere was a great entrepreneur who used his God-given talents to make money and help others. He built three types of Treasure Builders:

- **A business based on an invention.**

- **A service business that made money by doing repairs for others.**

- **A goods business which sold equipment.**

Now you know the **Clue**.

○ **Treasure Builders make money by selling inventions, services, and goods.**

If any of you needs wisdom, you should ask God for it. God gives freely to everyone and doesn't find fault.
— James 1:5 NIRV

Get all the advice and instruction you can, so you will be wise the rest of your life.
— Proverbs 19:20 NLT

Seek Wisdom

Knights, did you know that wisdom is free? If you want to be wise, read the Bible and seek wisdom from God and others. It is **The Kingdom Code** way!

Treasure Seeking

You have learned how an entrepreneur can build a business: with an invention, a service, or a goods business. Now, picture this. When all those businesses are in one area, they form an **economy** (ē-**kon**-uh-mē). An economy is the way goods and services are made, sold, and bought in an area.

Let's look at how goods and services are bought and sold in the United States by studying the American economy.

The American Economy Has Two Systems.

Capitalism (**ka**-pi-tl-iz-um) is a system where the people, not the government, have the right to start, own, and manage a business to make money.

In capitalism, people have the chance to have their own private business. A private business can belong to one person or a group of people. In the United States, most of the businesses are private businesses.

With capitalism, owners of a private business enjoy many freedoms.

Owners of a private business can choose:

★ How many hours to work.

★ Who works for the company.

★ How much to pay employees (em-**ploi**-ēz).

★ How much to charge for goods and services.

To win customers, a private business must **compete** (kum-**pĕt**). Compete means to try to get or win something that someone else is also trying to get or win. A business must compete for customers by offering something people *want* at a price they are *willing* to pay.

Free enterprise (**en**-ter-prīz) is a system where private businesses compete with each other with little control by the government.

Inside the United States, the free enterprise system gives a private business the freedom to compete with other businesses.

A private business can compete by:

★ Lowering prices.

★ Having a special sale.

★ Offering a reward if the customer buys a product.

In countries which do not have a free enterprise system, the government usually owns most of the businesses, so there is no need for competition (kom-pi-**tish**-un).

Knights, you will want to compete in your service business. Have you ever competed with anyone? It could have been a card game or a tennis match. You really worked hard to win, right? **KCKs**, a private business really works hard to win too! For your new private business to grow, you will need to work hard to find customers and keep them happy.

✥ Share Your Thoughts ✥

Let's look at how the free enterprise system could work in your neighborhood. Imagine some kids who live on the same street selling lemonade on the very same day. Whose lemonade will customers buy?

1. Whose lemonade would *you* buy? Why?
2. What could make you change your mind so you would buy from the other stand?
3. To compete, what can each lemonade stand add or change to get more customers?

Capitalism gives you the right to own a business. You have the freedom to succeed in business because capitalism gives you the **opportunity** (op-er-**too**-ni-tē). Opportunity is a chance to do something. This means you can succeed or fail in your new business quest.

You take a risk, but either way you learn!

You learn what to do and what not to do to succeed in a business. **KCKs**, if you own a private business in the United States, you have the freedom to manage your business the way you choose.

Wow! **No wonder they call it the free enterprise system!**

Capitalism is about a person's freedoms. Free enterprise is about a business's freedoms.

The benefits of capitalism and free enterprise are:

⭐ The opportunity to own a private business.

⭐ The right to make choices.

⭐ The chance to make as much money as you can.

From: **Aunt Jimmi**

A **mentor** (**men**-tawr) is a trusted person who gives advice and teaches others. Aunt Jimmi is your **KCK** mentor. Let's read first her letter.

Dear Kingdom Code Kids,

Have you ever seen someone create a business? Well, I have! In 1974, my husband, Johnny, told me he wanted to start a rivet business. I didn't even know what a rivet was! Do you? Have you ever seen those little buttons on the sides of big semi-trailers? Those are rivets. They hold things together.

My husband was an entrepreneur who saw an opportunity to sell rivets. So with a scale, some rivets, and a pick-up truck, he started the business.

For many years, we had very little money, but we were happy. We were living the American dream of owning and running our own business. We worked hard to build our company and loved watching it grow.

I thank God for capitalism and the freedoms we have in the United States! You will soon have the same opportunity to build a business. I hope you enjoy building your new businesses as much as we have enjoyed building ours.

Have fun,
Aunt Jimmi

KCKs, your adventure is about to begin. You will start a private business to earn money. Your first business will be a **service** business where you are paid to meet the needs of others.

TREASURE BUILDER

If you choose wisely, you will need little or no money to start your Treasure Builder. To help you make good choices, ask God for wisdom, listen to the advice of others, and do your research. Good choices will make your business a success.

What do **KCKs** do with some of the money they make from their businesses? **KCKs** help others when they can.

Kingdom Code Kids Think Differently!

We manage our money wisely so we can help others.

Your quest is to build a service business that supplies what people want and are willing to pay money to have. Knights, look in your neighborhood for a service you can supply.

- Can you clean for someone?
- Can you walk someone's pet?
- Can you do lawn or garden work?

You just found the **Treasure**.

KCKs practice the free enterprise system as they build a business.

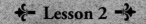

1. Complete #1-10 on *Activity 2: Research My Business* (behind *Activities* tab).

2. After completing #1-10 on *Activity 2,* use it to discuss each service business idea with your family. Talk about:

• Why each would be a good way to make money.

• Why each might not work.

• The help you may need.

• The time you will be able to work on your new business.

• Which business is the best choice for you and your family.

After discussing *Activity 2* with your family, file behind *Current Work* tab.

3. Use your flash cards to learn the Key Terms in Lessons 1 and 2. Save your flash cards to use again later.

4. Pick a business you want to own and manage. *Choose very carefully!* Have your family read and sign these two notices:

Notice 1: Treasure Builder Permit

Notice 2: Business Notice

Both of these notices must be turned in before you can start your business. When they are signed, place them behind *Current Work* tab in your KCK Binder. The two notices will be collected before Lesson 4.

Reminder!

Kingdom Keys

Key to the Lesson

In a free enterprise system, I can build a better business if I seek wisdom.

Key Ideas

Clue to the Code
Treasure Builders make money by selling inventions, services, and goods.

Character Code
Seek Wisdom

Treasure of the Kingdom
KCKs practice the free enterprise system as they build a business.

Key Terms

capitalism (**ka**-pi-tl-iz-um) a system where the people, not the government, have the right to start, own, and manage a business to make money

compete (kum-**pēt**) to try to get or win something that someone else is also trying to get or win

economy (ē-**kon**-uh-mē) the way goods and services are made, sold, and bought in an area

entrepreneur (ahn-truh-pruh-**noor**) a person who takes a risk to start and manage a business

free enterprise (frē) (**en**-ter-prīz) a system where private businesses compete with each other with little control by the government

mentor (**men**-tawr) a trusted person who gives advice and teaches others

opportunity (op-er-**too**-ni-tē) a chance to do something

 Complete *Worksheet 2: Prepare to Build Treasure.*
File behind *Treasure Builder 1* tab.

CONGRATULATIONS

You may place your Level Two reward on the KCK Treasure Map!

Bonus Code Work

1. Make a list of service businesses you see this next week. For example, you might see businesses on your way to school or in TV ads. On your list, place a check mark by those used by you or your family. Turn in your list.

2. Create a city showing an economy of many businesses. You can draw a map or make a 3-D model using blocks or other materials to build the city.

3. Practice counting money and making change. (*You may use scissors and paper to make your own play money.*)

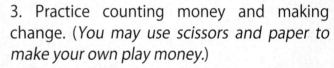

4. John Deere invented a plow that helped to make the farmers' work much easier. What invention do you think the world needs? On a poster, tell why the invention is needed. Draw a picture of what it would look like. Present your idea to the class.

Lesson 3

Entrepreneurs Build Businesses

Proclamation

The Lord has plans for me to succeed. His plans are to give me hope and a future.

Before you were born, God had a plan for your life. His plan was for you to succeed. Every day, you decide if you will follow His plan by the choices you make. You have a future filled with hope if you choose to follow God's plan.

Now, stand and repeat the *Proclamation*. While standing, put on the Armor of God.

Check Your Path

Begin *Worksheet 3: Entrepreneurs Build Businesses.*

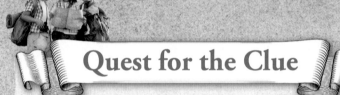

Quest for the Clue

Do you like to sing or listen to music? Most people do. Did you know during the 1800s American cowboys on long cattle drives would sing to their cattle to keep them calm?

You may not think walking a herd of cattle to sell them in a new area is a good business plan, but one American entrepreneur did. He made money doing it too! This entrepreneur was Charles Goodnight.

Mr. Goodnight was a cowboy who knew all about cattle. He started many businesses himself, and sometimes he had a partner. One of these partners, Oliver Loving, helped him start a great Treasure Builder.

They had the courage to blaze a 600-mile trail to move cattle from Texas to New Mexico, where they could sell their beef in a new **market** (**mar**-kit). A market is anywhere buying and selling can happen. What made them want to move cattle such a great distance?

In Texas, there were not enough people to buy all the ranchers' beef. So, the two men decided to move the cattle to places where beef was not available. It was a great idea, and capitalism gave them the opportunity to take this idea and start a new business. Their great idea became a huge Treasure Builder because of *supply* and *demand*.

Supply (suh-**plī**) is the amount of goods or services available to buy.

Demand (di-**mand**) is the desire and ability to buy goods or services.

Supply	**Demand**
Mr. Goodnight and other ranchers supplied the beef.	The people in New Mexico wanted beef.

KCKs, you need to understand supply and demand so your business can be a success. For example, when Goodnight and Loving took their cattle to a market where there was little beef, they probably got a high price for their beef. Why? The demand was very great. Over the years, more and more cattle were taken to New Mexico, so the price of beef probably went down. Why? The supply of beef was much higher. Knights, prices for goods and services go up and down because the demand goes up and down or the supply goes up and down. In economics, there is *The Law of Supply and Demand*. It is not a law you must obey; it is what usually happens in all businesses. How does *The Law of Supply and Demand* work?

The Law of Supply and Demand

The price of a product can change when the supply or demand for it changes.

For example, if the supply is less than the demand, prices usually go up.

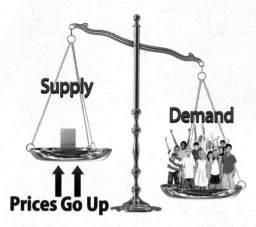

If Supply < Demand = Higher Prices

On the other hand, if the supply is greater than the demand, prices usually go down.

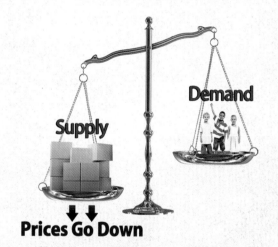

If Supply > Demand = Lower Prices

Brennan, a fifth grader, describes it this way, "If you have a lot of customers, but not enough supplies, you can increase your prices. If you don't have enough customers, but too many supplies, then you need to lower your prices."

Let's explore **The Law of Supply and Demand**.

⊰ Share Your Thoughts ⊱

Name something you and your friends would like to have. It might be a pair of tennis shoes, a type of jeans, a game, or a movie.

1. How much does the item cost now?

2. A year from now, do you think the price will be higher or lower? Why or why not?

3. Tell how this is an example of **The Law of Supply and Demand**.

Let's read more about Charles Goodnight.

Mr. Goodnight took many business risks. Most were a success, but in 1875, he set up a cattle ranch in Colorado that failed. Like a true entrepreneur, he had the courage to start over. He moved to Palo Duro Canyon in Texas where he started another cattle ranch.

After two years, he decided he could not manage the ranch by himself, so he chose another partner, John G. Adair. Together, they built a giant Treasure Builder called the *JA Ranch*. At one time, they had over 100,000 cattle on a million acres!

Can you guess what Mr. Goodnight did with a supply of cattle that large?

In 1877, Mr. Goodnight blazed a new cattle trail to Dodge City, Kansas, where he could sell beef in a new market. From Kansas, the railroads took the cattle to markets all over America. Mr. Goodnight's beef could be found on people's dinner tables all the way to the East Coast!

Did you find the **Clue** that made Mr. Goodnight a success?

 An entrepreneur takes a risk to start a business built on supply and demand.

Code of Honor

For God hath not given us the spirit of fear; but of power, and of love, and of a sound mind.

— 2 Timothy 1:7 KJV

Have Courage

You can have courage because God does not give you a spirit of fear! **KCKs**, look at the verse to find three things God does give you. As you begin your new Treasure Builder, always remember who gives you strength. With Christ on your side, fear does not have a chance to hold you back.

Treasure Seeking

Are you excited about becoming an entrepreneur?

An entrepreneur can be his or her own boss. That sounds pretty good! On the other hand, an entrepreneur takes risks and *wears many hats* to build a business. *Wearing many hats* means doing all types of jobs to make the business succeed.

Remember Aunt Jimmi's letter? What did Johnny do when he started the rivet business? He had to *wear many hats* because he bought all the products, delivered all the rivets, and then managed the money all by himself.

Knights, you will *wear many hats* as you build your Treasure Builders too. You will have the freedom to make choices and the opportunity to try new things. The free enterprise system gives you both of these benefits.

Choice and Opportunity

Mr. Goodnight had the same freedoms: **choice** and **opportunity**. Later in life, he had the opportunity to invest in a silver mining business in Mexico. It was not a good choice. Because of this decision, he lost $400,000!

God gave him knowledge (**nol**-ij) to succeed in the cattle business, but Mr. Goodnight chose to take a risk in a different business. What should you do before taking a risk? You can research, seek advice, and learn everything you can before you make a decision.

Kingdom Code Kids Think Differently!

Before taking risks, we research and seek advice to learn everything we can.

In the future you will have opportunities to take risks. Taking a risk is not always a bad thing to do; but before you take a risk, always remember to discuss it with others and do research. Ask God to guide and help you make the right choices. As an entrepreneur, you will make many decisions in your new business.

A — Let's see what qualities (**kwol**-i-tēz) an entrepreneur has. Complete *Activity 3: Become an Entrepreneur!* You may be surprised to find how many qualities you already have.

Knights, in order for you to succeed in your business, you may want to get advice from other people. Do you know someone who would be willing to help you?

You Need a Mentor!

Choose someone:

- You can trust.

- Who can teach you.

- Who gives you good advice.

In *On Your Own*, you will be asked to choose a mentor. Can you think of an adult who could help you make good decisions? Most business people have mentors to help guide them. Before making important decisions, successful people listen to their mentors' advice.

 Complete the first page of *Notice 3: Find a Mentor*. File behind *Current Work* tab until finished.

✦ History Highlights ✦

Have you ever thought about how something that happened a long time ago may have changed your life?

Imagine (ih-**maj**-in) getting goods, such as food or clothing, from one place to another without trucks, trains, or airplanes. Think about moving goods over dirt roads in a wagon.

Before the expansion (ik-**span**-shun) or growth of the railroad system in America, fresh food could not be found in many areas. Roads were bad and wagons were slow, so there was not an easy way to get supplies from one place to another.

Most early Americans had to grow their own vegetables, raise their own cows and chickens, or live without them! They could not always go to the store to buy food from other parts of the country. The Goodnight-Loving Trail was important because it was the start of the modern transportation system. The trail was used to drive cattle across the country to provide people with beef.

A large city, like New York City, needed beef brought to its stores. It could not raise its own beef because it did not have the **resources** (**rē**-sors-is). Resources are an available supply to be used when needed. There was no land to raise cattle in New York City, but there were plenty of people who wanted a big, juicy steak!

The development (dih-**vel**-up-munt) of the railroad system changed the way people lived and ate. How? It transported beef and other goods from one city to another. Today with modern transportation, the whole world economy has changed. You can buy lamb from New Zealand and grapes from Chile. You do not have to grow your own vegetables or milk your own cows.

Changes in transportation have made the United States and the rest of the world more **interdependent** (in-ter-di-**pen**-dunt), which means people or things that depend on each other. Both transportation and the world economy have been changed by inventions people made. **KCKs**, you have the same opportunity to change the world.

God's plan for you may be to change the way people live in the future.

You have discovered the Treasure.

An entrepreneur wears many hats and seeks advice from a mentor.

On Your Own

1. After the first page is signed, complete the second page of *Notice 3: Find a Mentor*. When complete, bring *Notice 3* back to class and file behind *Current Work* tab. Turn in before Lesson 6.

2. You will soon be using money in your service business. Practice counting money with your family or friends. Give change for different amounts of paper money. For example, you are given $5.00 for your service that costs only $3.50. What change would you give in return?

3. **Important!** Turn in the two notices below. They must be signed.

Notice 1:
Treasure Builder Permit

Notice 2:
Business Notice

ON YOUR OWN

Kingdom Keys

Key to the Lesson

I am an entrepreneur who has the courage to take risks and seek advice.

Key Ideas

Clue to the Code
An entrepreneur takes a risk to start a business built on supply and demand.

Character Code
Have Courage

Treasure of the Kingdom
An entrepreneur wears many hats and seeks advice from a mentor.

Key Terms

demand (di-**mand**) the desire and ability to buy goods or services

interdependent (in-ter-di-**pen**-dunt) people or things that depend on each other

market (**mar**-kit) anywhere buying and selling can happen

resource (**rē**-sors) an available supply to be used when needed

supply (suh-**plī**) the amount of goods or services available to buy

**Complete *Worksheet 3: Entrepreneurs Build Businesses*.
File behind *Treasure Builder 1* tab.**

CONGRATULATIONS

You may place your Level Three reward on the KCK Treasure Map!

Bonus Code Work

1. Do you want to know more about the Goodnight-Loving Trail? Check the library or the internet (*with your parent's permission*). Share what you learn.

2. Interview an entrepreneur to discover what demand was supplied in the business he or she built. List some of the problems that had to be solved for his or her business to succeed.

3. Draw a map of the Goodnight-Loving cattle trail. Show it to your class.

4. Choose something you can eat or use that comes from another country.

   A. Draw a picture or write a story to show where the item is grown or made.

   B. Imagine how the item travels to a store near you. Draw a picture showing the types of transportation used to get the item to you. For example: truck, ship, airplane, or train.

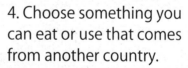

5. Use your flash cards to learn the Key Terms for Lessons 1-3. Keep the cards to use again.

Lesson 4

My Treasure Builder Plan

Proclamation

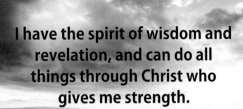

> I have the spirit of wisdom and revelation, and can do all things through Christ who gives me strength.

As you plan your business, ask God to send you **revelation** (rev-uh-**lay**-shun). Revelation is a new idea or greater understanding. **After all, God has the very best ideas, and He is waiting to share them with you. Always pray for God to send you wisdom and revelation so you can make good choices. Christ will give you the strength to reach your goals.**

Now, stand and repeat the *Proclamation*. While standing, put on the Armor of God.

Check Your Path

Begin *Worksheet 4: My Treasure Builder Plan.*

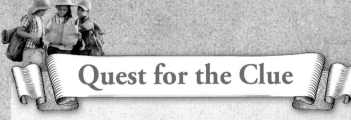

Quest for the Clue

Have you ever used a recipe to make cookies?

Have you ever planned a party?

Did you ever get a gift that needed to be put together?

To make amazing cookies, have a successful party, or build something correctly, what must you do first? You have to follow a plan. Your business needs a plan too. A **business plan** is a written plan telling how to start and manage a business. Let's read Aunt Jimmi's letter to find why it is important to have a plan.

On your mark!

Get set!

Charge!

Code of Honor

Be Prepared

Dear Kingdom Code Kids,

When I was young, I was a Girl Scout. I still remember our motto: Be Prepared. It didn't matter where we went or what we did, we always made a lot of plans.

Before a camping trip, we made long lists and talked about what to pack and how we would do everything. We might be stranded in the woods without toilet paper if we were not prepared!

Sometimes, it just seemed crazy to make so many plans, but you know what? It always paid off!

Writing a business plan for your new Treasure Builder is just like planning a camping trip. If you make plans, you will be prepared.

Even if planning seems boring, it is still the first step to making your business a BIG success.

Keep up the hard work. I know you can do it!

Until next time,
Aunt Jimmi

Suppose someone wants to build a tower. Won't he sit down first and figure out how much it will cost? Then he will see whether he has enough money to finish it. Suppose he starts building and is not able to finish. Then everyone who sees what he has done will laugh at him.

— Luke 14:28-29 NIRV

What is Aunt Jimmi trying to tell you? To run a successful business, you must *be prepared* by writing a business plan.

What do these verses tell you to do before beginning something? You need to know if you have enough money to finish what you start. That is **The Kingdom Code** way!

You found another **Clue**.

KCKs make plans so their Treasure Builders are successful.

Be prepared and plan ahead so you can always complete what you begin.

In order to build a successful service business, you need a great business plan. The better your plan is, the better your Treasure Builder will be. Seek wisdom from God so you can write the very best plan possible. Below are the five parts of your Business Plan.

Business Plan

Part A: Description of Business

Part B: Description of Service

Part C: Marketing Strategy

Part D: Financial Plan

Part E: KCK Extra Steps

You will complete **Part A** and **Part B** of your Business Plan in this lesson. You will fill in **Part C**, **Part D**, and **Part E** in Lesson 5. Now, let's read about **Part A** so you will understand what to do as you begin your Business Plan.

Part A: Description of Business

Part A of your Business Plan has seven steps. This is where you will write facts about your Treasure Builder.

A-1: Name of Business

In step **A-1**, you will write the business name you choose. **KCKs**, choose a business name that will catch people's attention and give them an idea of what service you are offering. For example, pretend your name is Gene, and you choose a trash can service where you offer to roll trash cans to the curb on trash day. A fun name could be...

Gene's Trash Take-Out

- **Choose a simple name.** Make sure it is easy to read and spell, easy to say and understand, and easy to remember.

- **Pick a name that is original** (uh-**rij**-uh-nl). Be sure no other business near you has the same name.

- **Choose a name so your business can grow.** For example, do not choose the name *Dog Walking* if you think you might want to sell dog collars later.

Be happy with the business name you choose!

A-2: Business Owner

Knights, you will soon be the owner of a **sole proprietorship** (sōl) (pruh-**prī**-i-ter-ship). A sole proprietorship is a business which is owned and run by one person. Guess what? You are that person.

You will be the owner of a sole proprietorship, and you will be the boss.

That is awesome!

A-3: Business Address

In this step, you write the business address where your customers can contact you.

A-4: Phone Number

You need a phone number where your customers can call to schedule (**skej**-oo-ul) a service.

A-5: Email Address

If you use an email for your business, you must check it every day. Answer emails quickly.

A-6: Hours of Operation

Hours of operation are the days and hours you can be contacted.

A-7: Total Minutes to Work Each Week

You need to know the total minutes you can work each week. Look at a calendar with your family. Discuss the days you can work and how much time you can work each day. Be sure you choose times when you do not have after-school activities or family events. See the example below.

> Kyle can work three days each week. On Monday he can work one hour. On Tuesday he can work an hour and a half. On Saturday he can work three hours and fifteen minutes.
>
> | | | |
> |---|---|---|
> | 1 hour | = | 60 minutes |
> | 1 hour + 30 minutes | = | 90 minutes |
> | 3 hours + 15 minutes | = | 195 minutes |
>
> Total minutes each week = 345 minutes

Fill in the blanks on your Business Plan.

- Use a pencil to complete each step.
- Put a small check mark beside any step you need to skip, and complete later.
- Erase the check marks after you complete the steps you skipped.

 Complete **Part A** on *Activity 4: Business Plan*. File behind *Current Work* tab.

> Before you use your last name, address, phone number, or email address in your business, discuss it with your family.

What is a survey?

A **survey** (**sur**-vā) is an activity to find what people think about something. You will soon conduct (kun-**dukt**) a customer survey of at least eight people to find:

• Who will use your service?

• Do people need or want your service?

• How much will people pay for your service?

Who will you survey?

In economics, every person you survey is called a **consumer** (kun-**soo**-mer). A consumer is a person who buys goods or services.

Consumers who might use your service are called **potential** (puh-**ten**-shul) customers. Potential means *possible* customers.

1. Who do you think might be potential customers for your business? Share ideas.

2. Write down all the names of your potential customers. You will soon use this list when you conduct your Customer Survey.

 3. Practice conducting a survey in class before you talk to potential customers. Use *Activity 5: Practice Survey*.

Now you are ready to talk to the people on your list, and conduct a real survey.

 Complete *Activity 6: Customer Survey*. File behind *Current Work* tab. You will use this activity in Lesson 5.

Be sure to get permission from your family to conduct your survey. Your family may want to be with you when you conduct your survey.

Part B: Description of Service

In **Part A** you described your business. Now, in **Part B** you describe your service.

B-1: Service Offered

In **B-1** you write all the services you offer in your business. For example, if you offer a lawn service, you might want to list: mow grass, trim bushes, pull weeds, plant flowers, and rake leaves. If you cannot trim bushes, do not list it. Knights, never tell a customer you can do something if you are not able to do it.

Kingdom Code Kids Think Differently!

We never promise something we cannot do.

B-2: Total Time to Do My Service

Find how long it takes you to do your service. Have someone time you.

Add extra time for the things below to find your total time:

- Pick up and put away supplies.
- Travel to and from the job.
- Talk with the customer and collect money.

You may want to ask your family or mentor to help you figure the *total time* it takes to complete your service from start to finish.

B-3: Selling Points

Selling points make people want your service.

✦ Share Your Thoughts ✦

To help you choose the best selling points for your Treasure Builder, discuss these ideas.

1. Name successful businesses in your area and tell what services they offer.

2. Why do people like these businesses? Do they supply customers' needs or wants?

3. What are you going to offer in your service business that is better or different from others? These are your main selling points.

Reasons People Use a Business = the Selling Points of the Business

A Complete **Part B** on A*ctivity 4: Business Plan*. File behind *Current Work* tab. If you take the Business Plan home, bring it back to class. It is used again in Lesson 5.

My Logo

A **logo** (lō-gō) is the symbol of a business. The logo can be a letter, a picture, or a special way a business writes its name. When you see a logo, it should remind you of a certain business. Let's think about this...

What is your favorite place to eat? Do you know its logo? Is the logo on the menu or on a big outdoor sign?

Knights, your business needs a logo too. You get to create your very own! Use your logo on posters, business cards, and flyers. You will show your logo to the class, so you may want to put the logo on a poster.

Paige's Pet Care

You will give a presentation (prez-un-**tā**-shun) of your Business Plan in Lesson 6. It will be fun to hear about other students' Treasure Builders as they share their Business Plans, too.

TERRIFIC

You have found the **Treasure**.

KCKs can write a business plan and create a logo.

REMEMBER

Activity 6: Customer Survey must be completed and returned to class before Lesson 5.

On Your Own

ON YOUR OWN

A. 1. Complete *Activity 7: My Logo*. File behind *Current Work* tab.

2. Your **KCK Sales Folder** will be used to keep papers for your new Treasure Builder. Write your name and phone number on your folder. You may want to put your logo, business name, or a picture of yourself doing your service on the front cover.

KCK

Kingdom Keys

Key to the Lesson

I am prepared to write a good business plan so my Treasure Builder is a success.

Key Ideas

Clue to the Code
KCKs make plans so their Treasure Builders are successful.

Character Code
Be Prepared

Treasure of the Kingdom
KCKs can write a business plan and create a logo.

Key Terms

business plan (**biz**-nis) (plan) a written plan telling how to start and manage a business

consumer (kun-**soo**-mer) a person who buys goods or services

logo (**lō**-gō) the symbol of a business

revelation (rev-uh-**lā**-shun) a new idea or greater understanding

sole proprietorship (sōl) (pruh-**pri**-i-ter-ship) a business which is owned and run by one person

survey (**sur**-vā) an activity to find what people think about something

 Complete *Worksheet 4: My Treasure Builder Plan.*
File behind *Treasure Builder 1* tab.

CONGRATULATIONS

You may place your Level Four reward on the KCK Treasure Map!

Bonus Code Work

1. Make a poster showing your logo, pictures, or information about your service business. Use this poster in your presentation.

2. Write a prayer asking God to give you revelation. You might ask for wisdom to write a great business plan or for courage to talk to potential customers. Think about what is the hardest part of beginning your new business, and ask God for revelation in that area.

3. Practice the sentence below. Try to say it faster than anyone else in your class.

"My Perfect Plan is to sell my service to all the Potential customers I Possibly can!"

4. With a partner, use your flash cards to see how many of the Key Terms you know from Lessons 1 - 4.

How to Create an Excellent Business Plan...

- ◆ Listen to your family and mentor.

- ◆ Pray for wisdom.

- ◆ Believe in yourself!

- ◆ Ask for advice from successful people.

- ◆ Dream big!

You hold the keys to your success.

KCKs Write
Great Business Plans!

Lesson 5

Business Plan Wrap Up

Proclamation

**My heart plans my way,
but the Lord directs my path.**

Have you ever made special plans, but things did not turn out as you thought they would? The next time this happens, try not to get upset or angry. God may have another path He wants you to take. Ask the Lord to direct your path as you complete your Business Plan and prepare your presentation. Now stand and repeat the *Proclamation*.

Check Your Path

W Begin *Worksheet 5: Business Plan Wrap Up.*

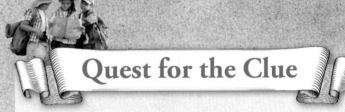

Quest for the Clue

Do you like to watch sports on television? Around the globe, more people watch the World Cup tournament (**tur**-nuh-munt) than any other sports event. In most countries, this sport is called *football*; but in America, it is called *soccer*. Let's look at what a coach does to get ready to compete in the World Cup.

A successful coach studies both his team and his competition (kom-pi-**tish**-un). He watches hours and hours of games so he can build a winning **strategy** (**strat**-i-jē). A strategy is a plan to reach a goal. A winning coach looks at how the other team plays. Then, he decides the best way to use the strengths of his own players to be better than the other team.

! **A coach's goal is to win games.
Your goal is to win customers!**

Knights, follow the example of a winning coach so your Treasure Builder will be a success.

Now you know the **Clue**.

🔍 **To be successful, KCKs know their strengths, study the competition, and have a winning strategy!**

I'm a KCK

Code of Honor

In the Bible, many people made their living by raising sheep and goats. The people took care of their flocks and protected them by being aware of every need the animals had. Why? The herd was their responsibility. **KCKs**, your new service business is totally your responsibility.

Be sure you know how your flocks are doing. Pay careful attention to your herds...
— Proverbs 27:23 NIRV

The shepherds had to carefully watch their herds and act quickly if their animals were sick or in danger.

Be Aware

You must be aware of any needs or problems in your business so you can take care of them quickly. That is **The Kingdom Code** way!

Treasure Seeking

One need all new business owners face is how to tell consumers about their new service. How do successful businesses do this? How do they get people to want their new service? They have a **marketing strategy**. A marketing strategy is a plan to tell consumers about a service or product. Knights, you need a marketing strategy too.

Challenge!

Create your own marketing strategy.

Part C: Marketing Strategy

The marketing strategy has three steps. Before you complete **Part C** of your Business Plan:

- Look at potential customers.
- Study the competition.
- Create **advertising** (**ad**-ver-tī-zing). Advertising is making people aware of an event, service, or product.

C-1: Potential Customers

As you know, a business will not succeed unless it has customers. In fact, they are the most valuable part of your business. Anyone who might use your service is a potential customer.

Think about your business. Do your potential customers own pets, have flower beds, or drive cars? You need to find the people who *need* or *want* your service. From your research and survey, you should have some idea of who your potential customers are.

C-2: Competition

To be better than your competition, you need to know what your competition offers and why consumers like to use them. How can you find this information? Research! You may go to the library, make calls, or talk to people to gather facts about your competition. **KCKs**, if you have no competition where you live, research businesses in other areas.

C-3: Advertising Plan

Advertising is a huge part of your marketing strategy because it lets people know about your business. Have fun as you create your advertising plan! Your plan should include where to advertise, what to put on ads, and what you can make or do that does not cost money.

Knights, your quest is to hunt and find free resources to use in your advertising. For example, old cardboard boxes can become yard signs, and construction paper or paper plates can be used to make flyers.

Kingdom Code Kids Think Differently!

We find and use free resources for advertising.

A Complete *Activity 8: Marketing Strategy Ideas.*

Part D: Financial Plan

Financial (fi-**nan**-shul) describes anything that has to do with money. Your financial plan is the strategy you choose to make and manage the money in your business. **Part D** has four steps to complete.

D-1: Price for Service

You need to know how much people are willing to pay for your service. If you know this, you can compete with your competition and have happy customers.

⚠️ **The price you choose for your service is one of the most important decisions you will make.**

📯 *Activity 9: Survey Results* should give you the price people are willing to pay. If it does not, you can call businesses in your area to see what price they charge. Talk to your family or mentor to find a fair price. Now, complete *Activity 9: Survey Results* using *Activity 6: Customer Survey.*

D-2: Start-up Capital

Capital (**kap**-i-tl) is money or property used in a business.

Remember the rivet business? When Johnny started the business, he had a pick-up truck and a scale. This property was part of his capital. The money he used to buy rivets and supplies was also part of his capital. Do you have tools, supplies, or money that can be capital for your new Treasure Builder?

The money or property that is used to start a new business is called *start-up capital.* **KCKs**, if you have money or supplies that you want to use in your new company, this will be your start-up capital. You can start a service business with or without capital. On the other hand, if you do not have any capital (money or property), but need supplies, you must find other ways to get what you need.

To be a successful entrepreneur in the business world, find and use things around you instead of spending money.

KCKs, in the last two steps of **Part D**, you set goals for your new business. After all, setting goals is part of a winning strategy.

For example if you want to catch a fish, you need to set a goal, make a plan, and go fishing!

D-3: Weekly Customer Goal

Your weekly customer goal is the number of customers your business can serve each week.

How to Find D-3: Weekly Customer Goal

Use the numbers you wrote on your Business Plan in **A-7: Total Minutes to Work Each Week** and **B-2: Total Time to Do My Service**. Copy the formula below on a piece of paper and fill in your numbers. Do the math to find your **D-3: Weekly Customer Goal**.

$$\underline{\hspace{2cm}} \div \underline{\hspace{2cm}} = \underline{\hspace{2cm}}$$
$$\text{A-7} \qquad\qquad \text{B-2} \qquad\qquad \text{D-3}$$

D-4: Weekly Income Goal

Your weekly income goal is the total amount of money you can earn each week.

How to Find D-4: Weekly Income Goal

Find the numbers you wrote on your Business Plan in **D-1: Price for Service** and **D-3: Weekly Customer Goal**. Copy the formula below on a piece of paper and fill in your numbers. Do the math to find **D-4: Weekly Income Goal**.

$$\$\underline{\hspace{1.5cm}} \times \underline{\hspace{1.5cm}} = \$\underline{\hspace{1.5cm}}$$
$$\text{D-1} \qquad\qquad \text{D-3} \qquad\qquad \text{D-4}$$

How can you reach your money goal?
You need to schedule (**skej**-oo-ul) a customer each and every time you can work.

Customers are the key to your success! Do not be upset if it takes you a while to fill up your calendar with customers. It takes time to build a business. Keep advertising and making sales calls until your calendar is full.

 Complete *Activity 10: Financial Planning*.

Part E: KCK Extra Steps

Extra steps turn a good team into a World Cup winning team. Extra steps are what make the difference between an OK business and a great business.

KCKs have amazing Treasure Builders because they take extra steps.

Choose your **KCK Extra Steps** from the ideas listed below. Later, you will write the ones you choose in **Part E**.

- I will be more organized.
- I will practice until it is easy to sell.
- I will research successful businesses.
- I will find new places to advertise.
- I will talk to my mentor every week.
- I will look for ways to grow my business.

You have discovered the **Treasure**.

A good marketing strategy and a strong financial plan help KCKs build a great business.

You are the leaders of tomorrow! Remember to follow God's plan for your life by making wise choices as you plan your new business.

REMEMBER

Lesson 6 is a review of Lessons 1 - 5. It is also when you will give your presentation.

Planning a Presentation

Complete *Activity 11: Helping Each Other Build Treasure*. After you understand what to do, file *Activity 11* behind *Current Work* tab.

1. Complete *Activity 4: Business Plan*. Use *Activities 6 - 10* if you need them. File *Activities 4 - 10* behind *Current Work* tab.

2. Finish making your advertising items. Save samples to show in your presentation.

3. Complete and turn in *Notice 3: Find a Mentor*.

4. Complete *Activity 12: Presentation Notes*. You will use *Activity 11: Helping Each Other Build Treasure* (behind *Current Work* tab). Place both *Activities 11* and *12* behind *Current Work* tab when complete.

5. Prepare for Lesson 6.

- Check to make sure *Activities 4 - 12* are behind *Current Work* tab.

- Have samples of your advertising items ready for your presentation.

ON YOUR OWN

Kingdom Keys

Key to the Lesson
I can reach my goals because I am aware of my strengths and have a winning strategy.

Key Ideas

Clue to the Code
To be successful, **KCKs** know their strengths, study the competition, and have a winning strategy!

Character Code
Be Aware

Treasure of the Kingdom
A good marketing strategy and a strong financial plan help **KCKs** build a great business.

Key Terms

advertising (**ad**-ver-tī-zing) making people aware of an event, service, or product

capital (**kap**-i-tl) money or property used in a business

financial (fi-**nan**-shul) anything that has to do with money

marketing strategy (**mar**-ki-ting) (**strat**-i-jē) a plan to tell consumers about a service or product

strategy (**strat**-i-jē) a plan to reach a goal

 Complete *Worksheet 5: Business Plan Wrap Up.*
File behind *Treasure Builder 1* tab.

CONGRATULATIONS

You have earned a Level Five reward for your KCK Treasure Map!

Bonus Code Work

1. What does *customer service* mean to you? Research to find what makes *good* customer service. Write a paragraph, create a power point presentation, or make a poster showing what you learned about giving good customer service. Share it with your class.

2. With a friend, practice counting money and making change until it becomes easy. Use the price you will be charging for your service. Take turns making change.

3. Practice giving your presentation by doing one of the following. Write what you learned from the experience. Turn it in.

- Using your notes, give your presentation in front of a mirror.

- Record yourself giving your presentation.

- Invite a family member or friend to watch you practice your presentation.

4. Find a Bible verse to encourage you as you write your Business Plan. Copy the verse and put it where you can see it every day.

Seek the Lord and His strength...
1 Chronicles 16:11a ESV

Lesson 6

Show What You Know

Proclamation

You have repeated five *Proclamations* since you began **The Kingdom Code**. Do you remember your favorite one? You will soon look back at each lesson and write your favorite *Proclamation* on *Worksheet 6*.

Check Your Path

This *Check Your Path* is also different because on *Worksheet 6* you will review Lessons 1 - 5. **KCKs**, it will be fun to see all the things you have learned in such a short time!

 Begin to answer questions on *Worksheet 6: Show What You Know.* You may use your book to find the answers.

⚜ Action Time ⚜

Are you ready to tell the class about your Treasure Builder?

Do you have everything you need for your presentation?

Soon you will listen to others' presentations. You will complete an Evaluation Card for each person. As you complete the Evaluation Card, give only **constructive** (kun-**struk**-tiv) **criticism** (**krit**-uh-siz-um). Constructive criticism means giving ideas to help others improve.

Knights, always look for good things you can say. If you have an idea that might improve someone's Treasure Builder, use kind words to share your thoughts on the Evaluation Card.

Treat others like you want to be treated. It is The Kingdom Code way.

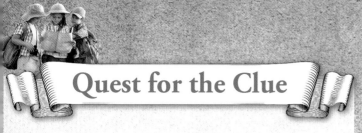

Quest for the Clue

Knights, let's review the **Clues** from the first five lessons.

Clue #1

The first **Clue** taught you about the Armor of God. Do you remember all the pieces?

THE **Belt** OF **Truth**

THE **Breastplate** OF **Righteousness**

THE **Shoes** THAT **Bring** THE **Message** OF **Peace**

THE **Helmet** OF **Salvation**

THE **Shield** OF **Faith**

THE **Sword** OF THE **Spirit**

KCKs, remember to put on the Armor of God every day for protection. If you are in the Armor of God, you are ready to fight anything that tries to keep you from being a leader in God's army!

Clue #2

Your second **Clue** taught you three types of businesses. Can you remember them?

3 Types of Businesses:

Inventions
Services
Goods

Clue #3

The third **Clue** came from Mr. Goodnight. He built a successful business because he saw a need and supplied it. Do you remember what he supplied?

Challenge!

KCKs, be able to describe how The Law of Supply and Demand works.

The Law of Supply and Demand

If supply is large and demand is small, prices usually go down.

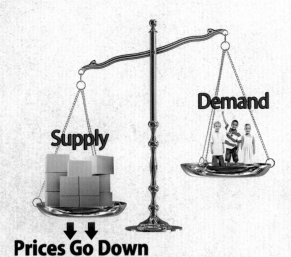

Prices Go Down

If Supply > Demand = Lower Prices

If supply is small and demand is large, prices usually go up.

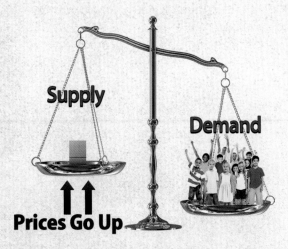

Prices Go Up

If Supply < Demand = Higher Prices

Clue #4

For the fourth **Clue**, you learn to plan ahead and be prepared. You think about the future so you are ready for whatever might happen. Being prepared is **The Kingdom Code** Way.

Clue #5

The fifth **Clue** told about a successful coach. To follow his example, what three things must you do?

How to Win!
Study the Competition.
Know Your Strengths.
Have a Winning Strategy.

You have found the **Clue**.

KCKs review what they have learned.

Code of Honor

A wise man will hear, and will increase learning...

— Proverbs 1:5a KJV

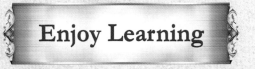

Enjoy Learning

To be wise, you should listen to others and learn from them.

 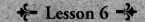

Kingdom Code Kids
Think Differently!

**We believe
learning is fun.**

Look around you. Be a sponge and soak up as much knowledge and information as you can. Knights, enjoy learning new things. If you enjoy learning, you will never be bored. Life will always be interesting.

Treasure Seeking

Let's read a true story about an interesting person from the past.

History Highlights

Joan of Arc was a French girl who became famous by hard work and **perseverance** (pur-suh-**veer**-uns). Perseverance means to continue trying even if it is difficult.

When Joan was a young girl, the enemies came many times and tried to take over her country. Even before she knew how to fight, she made up her mind to one day lead her people to victory!

Joan prayed for God to guide her. She began to study combat and military skills. By the time she was sixteen, she was battle-ready and prepared to lead an army! It took a long time and a lot of hard work to learn the ways of a knight, but she met her goal.

Joan went to the king to tell him she was ready to lead the army, but the king did not believe her. First, she had to prove to him that she was battle-ready. Only then, did the king trust her to lead the army to victory.

The king gave her control of the army, but God gave Joan perseverance.

She was a simple farm girl who put on the armor of a knight and led her people in battle. With practice and perseverance, Joan learned all the skills needed to win the victory. With perseverance, you can become a leader like Joan of Arc!

You have found the **Treasure**.

With practice and perseverance, KCKs can become leaders in the business world.

Kingdom Keys

Key to the Lesson

I will enjoy learning and show perseverance by reviewing what I have learned.

Key Ideas

Clue to the Code

KCKs review what they have learned.

Character Code
Enjoy Learning

Treasure of the Kingdom
With practice and perseverance, **KCKs** can become leaders in the business world.

Key Terms

constructive criticism (kun-**struk**-tiv) (**krit**-uh-siz-um) giving ideas to help others improve

perseverance (pur-suh-**veer**-uns) to continue trying even if it is difficult

**Complete *Worksheet 6:
Show What You Know.*
File behind *Treasure Builder 1* tab.**

**KCKs learn
to be leaders
by serving others.**

CONGRATULATIONS

You have earned a Level Six reward for your KCK Treasure Map!

Bonus Code Work

1. Give your presentation at a garden club or service club. This is a great way to advertise and get the names of potential customers.

2. Talk to your mentor about:

- Other places to advertise.
- How to manage your time better.
- Things that make a business successful.
- What to do in your business when the seasons change.
- Reaching your goals.

Write a paragraph or draw a picture to show what you learned from your mentor.

3. Write a skit and act it out for others. Use one of these ideas, or make up your own. Show:

- A crazy service business run by animals.
- Customer service.
- How supply and demand works.
- Competition between two businesses.

4. Discuss examples of **The Law of Supply and Demand** in your life. Talk about:

- Candy on sale after Valentine's Day.
- A game or toy you wanted, but could not get because the store sold out.
- A warm coat in the summer.

Think of more examples. Then, choose one example of how supply and demand affects your life. Make a poster showing your example, or write about it.

Lesson 7

How to Make a Sale

Proclamation

I will be bold because God gives me strength.

Knights, are you shy sometimes? Is it hard for you to raise your hand and speak up, even when you know the answer? The next time you are afraid, remember who gives you courage to be bold.

Now, stand and repeat the *Proclamation*. Put on the Armor of God for protection.

Check Your Path

Begin to answer questions on *Worksheet 7: How to Make a Sale.*

Dear Kingdom Code Kids,

You are starting a new business, and I am so proud of you! I want to tell you about the business I started where I became known as The Rivet Lady.

While Johnny sold rivets, I stayed at home all day painting pictures to sell. After a while I got very lonely, so every night I would ask Johnny tons of questions about his business. Finally, he said, "As much as you like to talk, I'll bet you could sell rivets over the phone!" Well, he planted an idea in me.

I took that idea and began to read everything I could find about telephone sales. Then, I learned about rivets from Johnny. He was my mentor. After a year of research and study, I decided to try selling rivets over the phone.

It was not as easy as I thought it would be. My first telephone sales call was terrible. My hands were sweating and shaking. I was so nervous, I even forgot my phone number.

Guess what? After a few calls, I realized the person talking to me could not see how nervous I was, so I began to feel better. I even practiced in front of a mirror to make sure I smiled. You might not believe this, but I practiced so much, it finally got to be fun.

Knights, make sales calls until it becomes easy. I know you can do it!

Take care,
Aunt Jimmi

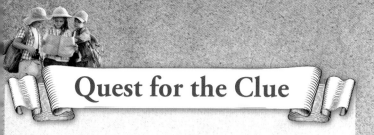

Quest for the Clue

As Aunt Jimmi made sales calls, she learned five secrets that helped her succeed.

1. • **Smile while you are talking.**

2. • **Know all about what you are selling.**

3. • **Keep important information close, where you can find it quickly.**

4. • **Practice until it becomes easy to do.**

5. • **Do not quit calling until you reach your goal.**

If you practice these secrets, you will build your **confidence** (**kon**-fi-dents). Confidence is believing you can succeed. **KCKs**, you may not think you can do something well at first, but with time and practice, you will get better. For example, remember the first time you tried skating, riding a bike, or swimming? Over time, did you improve and gain confidence?

 When you are confident, you believe in your heart you can do something well.

The KCK Calendar

Knights, before you begin selling, you need to make a calendar. This will help you keep track of each **appointment** (uh-**point**-munt). An appointment is a plan to be somewhere at a set time and date. You will write the days and times on your calendar when each customer wants to use your service. Let's make a **KCK Calendar** for this year, beginning with this month. For example, if this month is April, your calendar will start in April.

KCK Calendar

Five Steps to Make Your KCK Calendar

1. Find a current calendar to use as a guide.

2. Remove only one page of your **KCK Calendar** from behind *Forms/Notices* tab.

3. Write the month and your name.

4. Look at a current calendar. Copy the days of the month. Be sure to write number 1 in the same space and day on your **KCK Calendar**. *Remember, the first day of the month can begin on any day of the week.*

5. Check your **KCK Calendar** to make sure it matches the current month.

Complete the other eleven months the same way you did this month. Follow the same five steps. Then, put the months in order, starting with *this* month. Staple the pages together. Keep your calendar in your **KCK Sales Folder**.

Now you know the **Clue**.

 KCKs are successful because they prepare well, practice often, and believe in themselves.

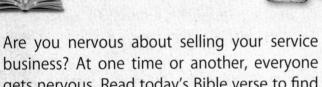

Code of Honor

Are you nervous about selling your service business? At one time or another, everyone gets nervous. Read today's Bible verse to find what happened to a man who was afraid and cried out to God.

When I called, you answered me. You made me bold by strengthening my soul.
— Psalm 138:3 NOG

Show Boldness

What can you do to show boldness as you contact potential customers?

• Ask the customer to make an appointment.

• If people say they do not want your service, do not give up. You should make another sales call right away.

• Keep making sales calls even if it is hard.

Kingdom Code Kids Think Differently!

We know God is always with us to help us be bold.

Believe in yourself!

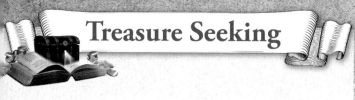

Treasure Seeking

KCKs, you have learned so much. You know **The Kingdom Code** is the way to make and money God's way.

- You have a great service to offer.
- You have a super advertising plan.

Ready to make a sale?

On your mark!

Get set!

Charge!

To help you make sales, the **KCK Sales Code** is just what you need. This code is a set of rules to give you confidence when you contact people. The code tells you how to be a **professional** (pruh-**fesh**-uh-nul). A professional is a person who is an expert in his or her work. Professionals learn many skills and try to improve the way their job is done. They work hard to be the best at what they do so they can succeed and be a winner.

To be a professional, remember the word...

LAPS

Look Good!
Act Awesome!
Pay Attention!
Speak With Confidence!

 Look good! Before you leave your house, look in a mirror and ask, "Will everyone be comfortable when they see me?" If your answer is "Yes," then you are ready to make a sale.

 Act Awesome! Smile, be happy, and use good manners.

 Pay Attention! Look into people's eyes. Listen carefully to what they say.

 Speak with Confidence! Practice making sales calls in front of a mirror. Ask yourself, "Do I sound confident? Do I speak clearly?" If not, continue to practice.

Do your **LAPS** to always make a super **first impression** (im-**presh**-un). A first impression is what people think about another person the first time they meet. When people first meet you, they form an idea of who you are in their minds. This is how they remember you. Professionals try to make a good first impression when they meet someone.

 Be a professional!

Knights, read *Activity 13: My KCK Sales Code.* Before you make a sales call, always go over the checklist on the back. Keep the sales code in your **KCK Sales Folder**.

Action Time

Three Types of Sales Calls

1. **Telephone Sales** = sales you make over the phone

2. **Face-to-Face Sales** = sales you make when you are looking at someone

3. **Written Sales** = sales you make using emails, notes, or flyers

> When making face-to-face sales calls, always have an adult with you. Get permission before you make written or telephone sales.

Knights, let's practice making each type of sales call.

Telephone Sales

To practice making telephone sales calls, you will need:

• *Activity 14: Telephone Sales Calls*

• Your **KCK Calendar**

• *Customer Sales Forms*

When complete, place *Activity 14* in your **KCK Sales Folder** to use as a guide when you make telephone sales calls.

Face-to-Face Sales

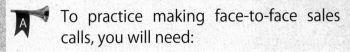

To practice making face-to-face sales calls, you will need:

• *Activity 15: Face-to-Face Sales Calls*

• Your **KCK Calendar**

• *Customer Sales Forms*

When finished, put *Activity 15* in your **KCK Sales Folder** to use as a guide.

Written Sales

Written sales are a great way to contact potential customers, but you must **follow up** (contact them again) until you know if they *do* or *do not* want your service. Never wait more than a week to follow up.

Knights, complete *Activity 16: Written Sales*. When finished, put *Activity 16* in your **KCK Sales Folder** to use as a guide when you write to a potential customer.

Set Your Goal

Knights, there is one more step to take before you start selling. You need to set a goal of how many sales calls you will make each week. These sales calls can be made in person, on the phone, or written. You may want to discuss with your mentor the best way for you to sell your service.

 Be sure your KCK Calendar and blank *Customer Sales Forms* are in your KCK Sales Folder to use when you make sales calls.

You may choose to keep all your completed *Customer Sales Forms* together in a special folder or binder, so you do not lose any of them.

Guess what? You have found the **Treasure**.

 KCKs can make three types of sales calls.

 1. Knights, complete your full 12-month **KCK Calendar**, if it is not already done. Keep it in your **KCK Sales Folder**.

2. Before you begin selling your service:

- Decide how many sales calls you will make each week, and write it on a piece of paper.

- Review the **KCK Sales Code**.

- Make sure you have your **KCK Calendar** and blank *Customer Sales Forms* available.

- When you make a sale, complete a *Customer Sales Form* and write the appointment on your calendar. Look at the example below.

Monday		Tuesday	
9	4-Mr. Poe 4:30-	10	4- 4:30-Jason

3. **Sell! Sell! Sell! KCKs**, it is time to post, send, or use your advertising to get customers.

 Be sure to put all your business money in your **Business Money Keeper** after you are paid.

Take your KCK Sales Folder home to start building your business!

Kingdom Keys

Key to the Lesson

With practice, I am prepared to boldly make sales calls.

Key Ideas

Clue to the Code
KCKs are successful because they prepare well, practice often, and believe in themselves.

Character Code
Show Boldness

Treasure of the Kingdom
KCKs can make three types of sales calls.

Key Terms

appointment (uh-**point**-munt) a plan to be somewhere at a set time and date

confidence (**kon**-fi-dents) believing you can succeed

first impression (furst) (im-**presh**-un) what people think about another person the first time they meet

professional (pruh-**fesh**-uh-nl) a person who is an expert in his or her work

KCKs, we can begin selling and earning money!

 Complete *Worksheet 7: How to Make a Sale*
File behind *Treasure Builder 1* tab.

CONGRATULATIONS

Place your Level Seven reward on the KCK Treasure Map!

Bonus Code Work

1. Make notices with *tear-off tabs* to advertise your business. Tear-off tabs make it easy for people to get your information. You need paper, ruler, and markers. You also need push pins, tape, or a stapler. Include your business name, telephone number, and what your service is. Put the notices in places where people go who might use your service. Have fun finding special places to put your notices.

Paige's Pet Care
Special Care for Your Special Pal

Tel: 123 456 7890
PetCare@go.let

I'll feed, wash, or walk your pet.

Paige's Pet Parade
123 456 7890

2. Form groups, or make a chart by yourself. With your group or classmates, discuss the three ways to make sales calls: *Telephone*, *Face-to-Face*, and *Written*. Write reasons you would use each one. List the challenges with each type of sales call. Then, choose the best ways to sell your service.

3. Look up Philippians 4:13. Copy it onto a card, and read it before you make a sales call. You can keep it in your **KCK Sales Folder**.

Lesson 8

Are Your Books in Order?

Proclamation

Listen as your teacher reads the *Proclamation* to you.

In my life and business, I will do everything in a proper and orderly way.

That is The Kingdom Code way!

Now, ask yourself some questions:

• Do I finish my chores?

• Do I keep my room clean?

• Do I complete my schoolwork?

• Am I organized (**or**-guh-nīzd)?

Check Your Path

W   Begin *Worksheet 8: Are Your Books in Order?*

Quest for the Clue

Let's imagine...

The alarm clock goes off. You stumble out of bed. Your clothes are on the floor. Your mom asks you to hurry and get dressed. **The Kingdom Code** logo is due today. You can only find one of your shoes. Your lunch box still has yesterday's leftover sandwich in it. The clock says 7:30, and you need to leave for class by 7:35! What are you going to do?

Does this ever happen to you? If it happens often, it is time for you to get organized! To be organized means you have a place for everything, and you always try to put everything back in its place. **KCKs**, if you have a plan and prepare for things to come, your life will run more smoothly.

Just as you need the Armor of God, you also need a **strategy** to organize your business.

STRATEGY

What will you need to make your strategy succeed? You will need your **KCK Calendar** and a **ledger**. A ledger (**lej**-er) is a record of the money a business has received or spent.

In your ledger, you will write down the money received in your business, which is called *income*. You will also write down every **expense** (ik-**spens**), which is money spent. Your **KCK Ledger** will keep track of all the money in your Treasure Builder.

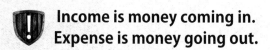

Income is money coming in. Expense is money going out.

Kingdom Code Kids Think Differently!

We plan ahead and keep track of our money.

You have found the **Clue**.

A calendar and a ledger help KCKs stay organized.

Code of Honor

Stay Organized

But be sure that everything is done properly and in order.
— 1 Corinthians 14:40 NLT

Do you think God is organized? Well, He is! He planned how He would make the world, and then He did it. God wanted order in His world. After He made it, He gave His people laws to obey and the Ten Commandments to follow. The Ten Commandments are God's code of rules that tell you how to treat others and honor Him. You can read them in Exodus 20:1-17.

✦ Share Your Thoughts ✦

1. Name some of the Ten Commandments that keep order in the world.

2. What are things you do each morning and night to help the day run smoothly?

3. Share secrets of how to organize your room, your things for school, and supplies for your activities.

4. Where are some places you keep things so you can find them quickly?

Treasure Seeking

Look back at the great things you have done. Knights, you have built a sole proprietorship *from the ground up.* You did research to find a Treasure Builder. Next, you learned how to sell your service by advertising and making sales calls. Then, you began contacting potential customers and setting appointments. You are on your way to building great treasure with your new Treasure Builder.

Congratulations! You are becoming an amazing entrepreneur.

You Have Done a Super Job!

Follow these four steps to become a winner and make money.

Be aware!

Be prepared!

Be financially responsible!

Be organized!

Knights, these steps will help you look and act like a professional. Let's take a closer look at each step.

On your mark!

Get set!

Charge!

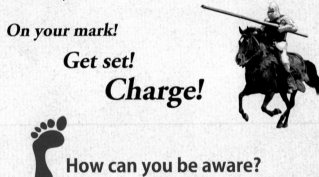

How can you be aware?

Check your calendar often so you do not miss an appointment. If you cannot be on time for an appointment, follow these steps:

- **Contact the customer.**
- **Apologize** (uh-**pol**-uh-jīz).
- **Tell the person when you will arrive.**

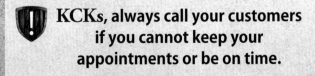

KCKs, always call your customers if you cannot keep your appointments or be on time.

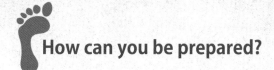

How can you be prepared?

Always have supplies you need for your service business ready to go. For example, if you wash cars, always have soap, sponges, dry towels, or anything else you need to do your job.

Use a sales backpack or tote bag to keep all your business supplies. Know where it is so you can grab it quickly. Put the following things inside this bag...

Pencils

Keep several sharp and ready to use.

Business Cards and Flyers

Always keep a few cards or flyers to give to customers. If you keep them in a clear, plastic bag, they are easy to find.

Business Wallet or Purse

This is the place to put the money you earn in your business.

KCK Sales Folder

Have your **KCK Calendar**, *Customer Sales Forms*, and **KCK Ledger** inside the folder.

Receipt Book

A receipt book has **receipts** (ri-sēts). A receipt is a written record showing something given and received. You will give each customer a receipt every time you are paid for a job.

Thank You Notes

Keep a few thank you notes in a clear, plastic bag. Give one to each new customer as soon as you are paid for your first job.

As soon as possible, put the money you earn in your Business Money Keeper. Never mix your business and personal money.

Saying thank you is part of a winning strategy.

Let's review the things that should be in your sales backpack or tote bag. If you remove any of these things, be sure to put them back.

1. **Pencils**
2. **Business Cards or Flyers**
3. **Business Wallet or Purse**
4. **KCK Sales Folder**
5. **Thank You Notes**
6. **Receipt Book**

Complete *Activity 17: Thank You Notes*. Keep in your **KCK Sales Folder**.

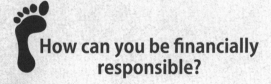

How can you be financially responsible?

Always remove the money from your wallet or purse. Put the money in your **Business Money Keeper** when you come home from a job. It will keep you organized.

Be sure to fill out your ledger every time money is received or spent in your business. It is super important for you to keep track of your money.

Remember when you read about *wearing many hats*? Well, get ready to put on another hat! You will now become a bookkeeper. A bookkeeper's job is to keep a ledger.

When you keep a ledger, you know if you have made a **profit** (**prah**-fit) or a **loss** (los).

A **profit** is when a business has more income than expenses.

A **loss** is when a business has more expenses than income.

Be a winner! Keep an up-to-date ledger.

This is what the top part of your KCK Ledger looks like.

 # KCK Ledger

Business Name: _____ Business Owner: _____

	Date	Description	Income + (Money In)			Expenses – (Money Out)			Balance = (Money on Hand)		
1		Beginning Balance									
2											

KCKs, let's look at the words on your **KCK Ledger**. Then, let's learn what to write in each column.

A **transaction** (tran-**zak**-shun) is an event where money is transferred. Every time a business spends or receives money, a transaction takes place. This information must be written in your ledger.

When you write this information in your ledger, you make an **entry** (**en**-trē). An entry is a written record in a ledger that gives important details about a transaction. When you make an entry, always use a pencil so you can erase your mistakes.

1. Look at the ledger above. The **Date** is the first thing you write when you make an entry. The date is when the transaction happens. It is the date the money *comes in* or *goes out*.

2. The **Description** (dih-**skrip**-shun) is written in the second column. You enter to *whom* the money was given or *from where* the money came. Then, you write why the money *comes in* or *goes out*.

3. The third column is where you enter money that *comes in*. The **Income** column has a *plus* sign because this money is added.

4. The fourth column is where you enter the money that *goes out*. Always use a red pencil when you write in the **Expenses** column. This column has a *minus* sign, because this money *goes out* and is subtracted.

5. The last column is your **Balance**. To finish your entry, use your last balance and add the income or subtract the expense to get your new balance. The new balance now becomes the amount of money you have on hand. If your ledger is up to date, your **Balance** should always be what you have in your **Business Money Keeper**. Now that you know the steps to make an entry, let's look at Emma's ledger.

This is Emma's ledger below. Let's see how she enters her first transactions.

Business Name: <u>Emma's Babysitting Service</u>　　　　Business Owner: <u>Emma Brown</u>

	Date	Description	Income + (Money In)			Expenses − (Money Out)			Balance = (Money on Hand)		
1	5/16	Beginning Balance								0	0 0
2	5/17	Mrs. Green - babysitting	1	0	0 0				1	0	0 0
3	5/18	AB Office Store - thank you notes					2	0 0		8	0 0

1. Look at line one. Emma wrote the date, May 16, as 5/16 in the first column. She wrote 5 for May, because it is the fifth month of the year; she wrote 16 for the day of the month. Notice, she put zero in the **Balance** column because Emma had no money when she started her service business.

KCKs, how much start-up capital do you have? This is the amount you will enter for your beginning balance when you start keeping your ledger. It might be zero, like Emma's.

2. Look at Emma's second entry. She received $10 on May 17 for babysitting. Emma wrote:

5/17 = **Date**
Mrs. Green - babysitting = **Description**
$10.00 = **Income**

Then, Emma *added* the $10.00 in her **Income** column to her zero balance in her **Balance** column. Emma's new balance is $10.00.

$$\$0.00 + \$10.00 = \$10.00$$
$$\$10.00 = Balance$$

3. Look at her third entry. She entered the information just as before, except this time it was an expense. So, she entered $2.00 in the **Expenses** column. Did she use a red pencil?

Then, she *subtracted* the expense of $2.00 from the $10.00 in her **Balance** column. Emma's new balance is $8.00.

$$\$10.00 - \$2.00 = \$8.00$$
$$\$8.00 = Balance$$

4. Emma checked to make sure she had $8 in her **Business Money Keeper** to match the **Balance** in her ledger.

Balance = Amount in **Business Money Keeper**

Knights, begin your **KCK Ledger** entries as soon as you get or spend money in your Treasure Builder. When you start a new page in your ledger, always enter a beginning balance. After the first page, each new beginning balance is the last balance from the page before.

Reminder!

Be Organized!

1. **KCKs**, send a thank you note after the first time you provide a service for a customer. If you keep some thank you notes in your sales backpack or tote bag, you will be able to give one to the customer right away.

2. When you make appointments, be sure you write them on your **KCK Calendar.** Write the name of the customer beside the time you can do your service.

3. After you complete a job, replace supplies in your sales backpack or tote bag. You want to be ready for your next appointment.

You have found the **Treasure**.

KCKs know how to write a receipt, a thank you note, and make a ledger entry.

Before you begin your ledger, practice making some entries in Emma's ledger. Complete *Activity 18: What is Emma's Balance*?

On Your Own

1. It is time to start making entries in your **KCK Ledger** (behind the *Forms/Notices* tab). Write your name, business name, and beginning balance (your start-up capital) in your ledger. Take the ledger home, and put it in your **KCK Sales Folder**. Keep it up to date.

2. If you did not write the times you can work on your **KCK Calendar** in *Bonus Code Work* of Lesson 7, it is time to get organized! Remove your **KCK Calendar**.

• On the correct dates of your calendar, write the appointment times you can work. Leave space for the customer's name. See below:

	Monday		Tuesday	
9	4- 4:30-	10	4- 4:30-	

• Now, it will be easy to see where to write the customer's name on the calendar. As soon as you set a time to work, find the correct date, and write the customer's name next to the correct time. See below:

	Monday		Tuesday	
9	4-Mr.Poe 4:30-	10	4- 4:30-Jason	

Do not get discouraged. Hang in there! It takes time to get customers. You can do it!

Kingdom Keys

Key to the Lesson

With my calendar and ledger, I will stay organized so I can have a successful Treasure Builder.

Key Ideas

Clue to the Code
A calendar and a ledger help **KCKs** stay organized.

Character Code
Stay Organized

Treasure of the Kingdom
KCKs know how to write a receipt, a thank you note, and make a ledger entry.

Key Terms

entry (**en**-trē) a written record in a ledger that gives important details about a transaction

expense (ik-**spens**) money spent

ledger (**lej**-er) a record of the money a business has received or spent

loss (los) when a business has more expenses than income

profit (**prah**-fit) when a business has more income than expenses

receipt (ri-**sēt**) a written record showing something given and received

transaction (tran-**zak**-shun) an event where money is transferred

 Complete *Worksheet 8: Are Your Books in Order?*
File behind *Treasure Builder 1* tab.

 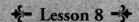

CONGRATULATIONS

Place your Level Eight reward on the KCK Treasure Map!

Bonus Code Work

1. Use your flash cards to review the Key Terms.

2. Read *The Ant and the Grasshopper.* Draw or write what this story tells you about working and saving for the future.

3. Thank you notes do not have to look boring. Get creative! Have fun making personalized thank you notes.

4. Are your school supplies and papers organized? Ask your family or teacher to help you get your school things organized in a way that will help you. At least once a week, make sure you are staying organized.

5. Interview two adults to find out what they do to remember appointments.

6. Use ideas learned in *Share Your Thoughts* to organize your room or closet. Make it is easier to get ready for your day.

7. You may have many activities, sporting events, lessons, and projects for school. To make sure you do not schedule job appointments when you have other plans, add your personal schedule to your **KCK Calendar**. For example, if you have baseball practice every Tuesday and Thursday from 3:00 to 5:00, write it down on your calendar. To make it easier, you can use letters, like **BP**, to record **B**aseball **P**ractice.

Lesson 9

A Money Plan

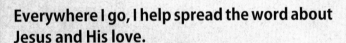

Proclamation

Everywhere I go, I help spread the word about Jesus and His love.

Read to find what Jesus promises and wants Christians to do.

Go ye therefore, and teach all nations, baptizing them in the name of the Father, and of the Son, and of the Holy Ghost: Teaching them to observe all things whatsoever I have commanded you: and, lo, I am with you always, even unto the end of the world. Amen.

— Matthew 28:19-20 KJV

Check Your Path

Begin *Worksheet 9: A Money Plan.*

Quest for the Clue

What do you do when you are thirsty?

1. **Get a glass.**
2. **Go to the sink.**
3. **Turn on the water.**

What do you do next?

You can choose to put the glass under the faucet, drink the water, and quench your thirst. Or, you can just let the water run down the drain, and you are still thirsty.

The very same thing can happen to your money.

You have a choice.

Knights, you can waste your money, and it will vanish; or you can use your money wisely.

You need a money plan!

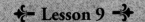

The **KCK** money plan can help you use your money wisely and be financially responsible. It shows you how to:

- **Divide up your money.**

- **Keep track of your money.**

- **Manage your money.**

For example, if you have personal money saved from gifts, jobs you did in the past, or your allowance (uh-**lou**-uns), the **KCK** money plan is a great way to manage it. In economics, a money plan is called a **budget** (**buj**-it). A budget is a plan used to decide how money will be spent. Knights, your money plan is called the **KCK Budget**.

Having a budget puts you in control of your money.

Kingdom Code Kids Think Differently!

We follow the KCK Budget to help us use our money wisely.

You will use the **KCK Budget** to split up your money into five parts. The five parts are: *Jesus, Others, Education, Yourself,* and *Savings.* After you divide your money into the five parts, you will put it into zippered pockets. These pockets are called *JOEYS Treasure Keepers.*

Each *Treasure Keeper* will be marked with a special letter: *J, O, E, Y,* and *S.* Just think of the word *JOEYS*, so you can easily remember the parts of the **KCK Budget**. Look at each part:

J - O - E - Y - S

 stands for *Jesus*

 stands for *Others*

 stands for *Education*

 stands for *You*

 **stands for *Savings***

In Lessons 9 – 13 you will learn about the **KCK Budget**. After Lesson 13, you can begin using your *JOEYS Treasure Keepers* for your personal money. If you do not have personal money, you will use your *JOEYS Treasure Keepers* after Lesson 27.

If I Budget My Money:

I can feel safe and secure.

I can be in control of my money.

I can stay out of debt.

I can have a bright financial future.

Knights, the **KCK Budget** can put you on the path to **financial security** (si-**kyoor**-i-tē). Financial security is having enough money for your needs now and for the future.

Way to Go!

You have found another **Clue**.

🔍 **KCKs use a budget to become great money managers.**

The earth belongs to the Lord. And so does everything in it. The world belongs to Him. And so do all those who live in it.
— Psalm 24:1 NIRV

You and everything you have belongs to God, including your money. He lets you use the money and things He gives you, but He wants you to be a good **steward** (**stoo**-erd). A steward is a person who takes care of something that belongs to someone else. As you take care of God's money, you can use it to help others.

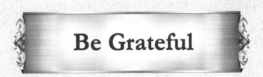

Be Grateful

Be grateful to God for everything. Take care of God's world and the things He gives you. That is **The Kingdom Code** way.

Challenge!

Be a good steward and show gratefulness by sharing your talents, money, and knowledge.

What else does the Bible tell you about being a good steward?

...From everyone who has been given much, much will be demanded; and from the one who has been entrusted with much, much more will be asked.

— Luke 12:48b NIV

Do you know what this verse means? It means the *more* you get from God, the *more* He expects from you. God blesses those who take care of His people and His things, but responsibility comes with God's blessings.

 The more God gives you, the more responsibility you have.

1. Think about your special talents and your money. How can you be a good steward and use your money and talents to show gratefulness to God and help others?

2. Does knowing that God owns *everything* change the way you look at what you have?

3. How does a church help others by using the money you give?

Treasure Seeking

J is for Jesus
J
10%

Knights, to be a good steward, it is important to give back to God *first*. That is why the first letter in the **KCK Budget** is a *J,* because *J* stands for *Jesus*.

There are verses in the Bible that tell how much God wants people to give back to Him. The Old Testament teaches you about giving God a **tithe** (tīth). A tithe is an offering for God, usually one tenth. The people in the Old Testament gave one tenth of everything God gave them.

Let's figure out how much one tenth really is. For example, you know one dollar is worth 100 cents. If you want to give one tenth of one dollar, you would give ten cents or one dime.

1/10 of a dollar = 10¢ or 1 dime

A dime is a tenth of a dollar (10/100 = 1/10) because there are ten dimes in one dollar. **KCKs**, to tithe means giving one dime out of every dollar to Jesus.

Another way to say one tenth is ten **percent** (per-**sent**). Percent means one part in a hundred (1/100 or 1%). One percent is 1/100, so to tithe ten percent is to give 10/100 or 1/10.

1/10 of 1 dollar = 10¢

Look at the circle below to see what the first part of your **KCK Budget** looks like.

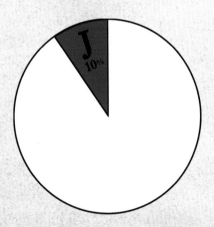

J **= 10% to *Jesus***

To find this amount, multiply 0.10 times the total amount of money you are dividing into your **JOEYS** *Treasure Keepers*. For example, if you have $15.00, you would multiply $15.00 times 0.10 to find 10%. Your answer is $1.50, so you would put $1.50 into your *J Treasure Keeper*. Every time you divide your money, use the formula below to find how much goes into your *J Treasure Keeper*.

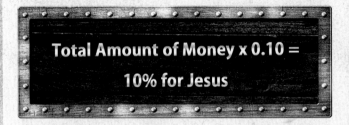

Total Amount of Money x 0.10 =

10% for Jesus

In the Bible, the New Testament tells you to give with a happy heart.

Everyone must make up his own mind as to how much he should give. Don't force anyone to give more than he really wants to, for cheerful givers are the ones God prizes.
— 2 Corinthians 9:7 TLB

Jesus gave His life for you. It pleases Him when you give back to Him. When you give ten percent of what you have, it is an offering to Jesus and should be given with joy.

You have found the **Treasure**.

KCKs put ten percent of their money into a *J Treasure Keeper*.

 Knights, do not put money from your Business Money Keeper into your *JOEYS Treasure Keepers*. Use only personal money.

Complete *Activity 19: Understand the Math of JOEYS*.

1. You started using the **KCK Sales Code** in Lesson 8. Now, let's learn the first rule. Say it until you know it.

My KCK Sales Code

1 **My hair, hands, body, and teeth are clean!**

2. If you have not finished your **KCK Calendar**, follow the five steps on page 53. Remember to staple the twelve months together, beginning with the current month. Keep your calendar in your **KCK Sales Folder**.

3. If you still have appointment times available on your calendar, make extra sales calls. Find new customers and schedule appointments.

4. Make follow-up sales calls to customers who do not have appointments. Fill in the Follow-up Report on the back of each *Customer Sales Form* as you contact them.

Kingdom Keys

Key to the Lesson
I am a grateful steward and give to Jesus with a happy heart.

Key Ideas

Clue to the Code
KCKs use a budget to become great money managers.

Character Code
Be Grateful

Treasure of the Kingdom
KCKs put ten percent of their money into a *J Treasure Keeper.*

Key Terms

budget (**buj**-it) a plan used to decide how money will be spent

financial security (fi-**nan**-shul) (si-**kyoor**-i-tē) having enough money for your needs now and for the future

percent (per-**sent**) one part in a hundred (1/100 or 1%)

steward (**stoo**-erd) a person who takes care of something that belongs to someone else

tithe (tīth) an offering for God, usually one tenth

God loves a cheerful giver.

Complete *Worksheet 9: A Money Plan.* File behind *Treasure Builder 1* tab.

CONGRATULATIONS

Place your **Level Nine** reward on the KCK Treasure Map!

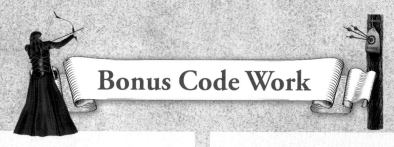

Bonus Code Work

1. Get a copy of the budget of a church. Draw pictures to show where the money is spent by that church.

2. Interview someone from a church to learn how that church uses money it receives. Write about the facts you find.

3. Be a good steward in your community. Clean up your neighborhood, or help others where there is a need.

4. Read a book or watch a movie about a missionary who told others about Jesus. Ask your parent, mentor, or someone from your church to recommend a missionary to study. Give an oral report, write a paragraph about this special person, or write the missionary a letter to learn more about what they do.

Lesson 10

O Stands for Others

Proclamation

I will treat others like I want to be treated.

How do you like to be treated? Are kindness, respect, sharing, and honesty important?

Now stand and repeat the *Proclamation*. While standing, put on the Armor of God. Then, take a moment to think about what the *Proclamation* means to you.

Check Your Path

Begin *Worksheet 10:*
O Stands for Others.

Quest for the Clue

It feels good to give and receive. Did you know that you have something to give to others every day without spending a single penny? When you give it away, it is often given back to you. Can you guess what it is?

Your Smile!

Knights, have you ever seen people whose faces seem to light up the room when they smile and talk? Their eyes sparkle and they laugh easily. They are often great givers who think of others first. They have learned that giving makes them happy inside and out. You can actually see their joy.

KCKs, you have the opportunity to be one of these people.

Challenge!

Spread joy by giving a free smile to everyone you meet.

Sometimes things can happen to people they do not expect. Maybe their homes are destroyed by fire, or they could have a terrible accident.

Disasters (di-**zas**-terz) can happen at any time, like the tsunami (soo-**nah**-mē) that hit Japan, or Hurricane Katrina that hit the United States. Earthquakes and tornadoes can cause great damage to homes and office buildings.

People may even be forced to leave their homes forever. Can you imagine being forced to leave your home with only minutes to grab your things and go? When disaster strikes, water and electricity are often not available.

At these times, just a glass of clean water can be hard to find.

A glass of water is such a simple gift, but it could be just what someone needs if a disaster happens. You might not be able to hand out water yourself, but your donation to a special group going to the disaster area can make a big difference.

Let your light shine so others will see Jesus in you and praise Him because of your **generosity** (jen-uh-**ros**-i-tē). Generosity is the act of giving something of value to someone else.

Let your light so shine before men, that they may see your good works, and glorify your Father which is in heaven.
— Matthew 5:16 KJV

Start at home with your family. Then, look for ways to help others in your community. Also, think about the men and women in our military who serve our country. They are willing to give their lives so you can be free!

KCKs, it is important to be aware of others' needs. It is even more important to *do* something about those needs. What can you give to others? Think carefully, and do it now!

Kingdom Code Kids Think Differently!

We look for opportunities to help others.

Dear children, don't just talk about love. Put your love into action. Then it will truly be love.

— 1 John 3:18 NIRV

 Knights, turn your ideas into actions by helping and giving to others.

It is **The Kingdom Code** way!

Be aware of the small things you can do. For example, if someone in front of you at the store needs a few more cents, help if you can.

If you cannot help financially, there are other ways you can show you care. One thing you can share is your **talent** (**tal**-unt). A talent is a special ability to do something very well.

God gives you talents which are always free to share. For example, you can teach others what you know. You can also help in the kitchen. When you see someone in need of your talents, jump to the rescue!

From: *Aunt Jimmi*

Dear Kingdom Code Kids,

I want you to be successful as you build your business. A customer once told my husband that our business is a success because all the people who work there have a sense of urgency.

The customer said when he orders rivets, everyone in the company seems in a hurry to get them to him as quickly as possible. Knights, when you see a need in your business, you should have a sense of urgency too. Rush to meet the needs of your customers, and you will succeed.

My mother was always quick to respond when she saw a need of any kind. Mom's talent was cooking. If a new baby was born, a new neighbor moved in, someone was sick, or a disaster struck, she went straight to the kitchen and started cooking. I cannot tell you how many cakes, pies, hams, and bowls of chicken and dumplings I have delivered for her. She would say, "We can't mess around; they need help right now!" Then, she went to work and rushed to get some food to those in need. KCKs, always have a sense of urgency! When you see a need of any kind, fill it quickly if you can.

Your mentor,
Aunt Jimmi

P.S. I was traveling to Dallas not long ago, and one of my tires had a blowout. A young man saw my problem, pulled over, and changed my tire. He saw a need and quickly filled it. What a great young man!

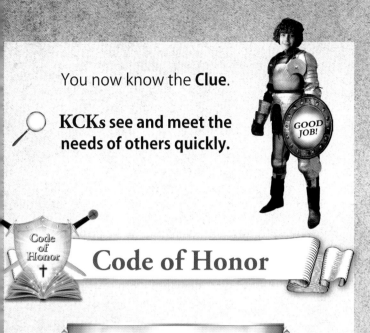

You now know the **Clue**.

🔍 **KCKs see and meet the needs of others quickly.**

Code of Honor

Show Generosity

Look for opportunities to give. Jesus tells us...

"I was hungry, and you gave me something to eat. I was thirsty, and you gave me something to drink. I was a stranger, and you took me into your home. I needed clothes, and you gave me something to wear. I was sick, and you took care of me. I was in prison, and you visited me.

"Then the people who have God's approval will reply to him, 'Lord, when did we see you hungry and feed you or see you thirsty and give you something to drink? When did we see you as a stranger and take you into our homes or see you in need of clothes and give you something to wear? When did we see you sick or in prison and visit you?'

"The king will answer them, 'I can guarantee this truth: Whatever you did for one of my brothers or sisters, no matter how unimportant they seemed, you did for me.'"

— Matthew 25:35-40 NOG

❧ Share Your Thoughts ❧

1. Tell how you can give to others with your:
   - Words.
   - Time.
   - Talents.
   - Things that belong to you.
   - Money.

2. What happens when you give to others? Read Proverbs 22:9 for a clue.

When you give to other people, Jesus says you are giving to Him. He can see everything you do, so always look for every opportunity to show generosity. **KCKs**, let your light shine. It is **The Kingdom Code** way!

FOOD DONATIONS

Treasure Seeking

From the last lesson, did you learn how important it is to have a money plan? Close your eyes and see if you can remember what each letter stands for in **JOEYS**.

J - O - E - Y- S

 stands for *Jesus*

 stands for *Others*

 stands for *Education*

 stands for *You*

 stands for *Savings*

Just think of the word JOEYS, and you can easily remember the five parts of the KCK Budget.

Knights, sometimes you may want to give to others because they are special to you. That is why the second letter in the **KCK Budget** is an *O*, because *O* stands for *Others*.

At special times, giving to someone is very **appropriate** (uh-**prō**-prē-it). Appropriate means right for the time.

For example, your grandfather's birthday, Christmas, or Mother's Day are all appropriate times to give. Would you like to have money to buy presents for these special times? Planning ahead can make it happen because you will put money into your *O Treasure Keeper*.

When you give to others, everyone is blessed.

God sees your generosity.

There will always be opportunities to help others, and you will not be able to meet all the needs you see. **KCKs,** sometimes you have to choose between giving to others and giving to members of your own family. It can be a tough choice to make. If members of your family have needs, they should always be considered first. Think about your own family. Then, reach out to others.

To help you be generous, five percent (5%) of your **KCK Budget** will be set aside for others. To find this amount, multiply 0.05 times the total amount of money you are dividing into your *JOEYS* Treasure Keepers. Remember, none of the money you earn in your business can be put into the *JOEYS* pockets. Your business money must stay in your **Business Money Keeper** until Lesson 27. Use the formula below to find how much money goes into your *O Treasure Keeper*.

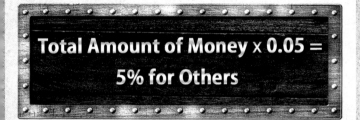

Total Amount of Money x 0.05 =
5% for Others

To give five percent to *Others*, look at the circle below to see what the second part of your **KCK Budget** looks like.

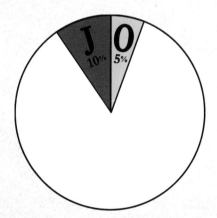

O = **5% to** *Others*

You have found the **Treasure**.

KCKs are blessed when they give five percent of their money to others.

1. Learn the second rule of the **KCK Sales Code**. Say it until you know it. You can practice with a friend.

My KCK Sales Code

2 | **I look into the other person's eyes when we talk to each other.**

2. Complete *Activity 20: Giving to Others*. Find a special place at home where you can keep this chart. It will remind you when to give gifts or remember others.

3. Look at your *Customer Sales Forms* in your **KCK Sales Folder**. Check the back of each form. If you need to schedule more appointments, make sales calls. If you still have appointment times available on your calendar, make extra sales calls to find new customers.

Kingdom Keys

Key to the Lesson

When I see a need, I show generosity and meet that need as quickly as I can.

Key Ideas

Clue to the Code
KCKs see and meet the needs of others quickly.

Character Code
Show Generosity

Treasure of the Kingdom
KCKs are blessed when they give five percent of their money to others.

Key Terms

appropriate (uh-**prō**-prē-it) right for the time

generosity (jen-uh-**ros**-i-tē) the act of giving something of value to someone else

talent (**tal**-unt) a special ability to do something very well

W Complete *Worksheet 10: O Stands for Others.* File behind *Treasure Builder 1* tab.

Use your talents to show generosity!

CONGRATULATIONS

Place your Level Ten reward on the KCK Treasure Map.

Bonus Code Work

1. Write a special card to encourage a friend or brighten someone's day.

2. Gather and send a care package to troops who are away from home or a missionary that your church supports. Include a note to encourage them.

 3. Are you good at math? Have fun with *Activity 21: Fun with Numbers.* Complete and file behind *Treasure Builder 1* tab.

4. Choose to be a good steward. Take care of something that belongs to someone else.

5. Is your special talent cooking or singing? Choose one of your talents, and share it.

Lesson 11

E Stands for Education

Proclamation

Listen as your teacher reads the *Proclamation*.

I am always ready to learn.

How can you be ready to learn? Listen and ask questions when you do not understand. **KCKs**, you must be willing to learn by having a good attitude. It is your choice. Now, stand and repeat the *Proclamation*.

Check Your Path

Begin *Worksheet 11: E Stands for Education*.

Quest for the Clue

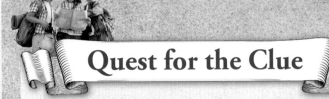

Knights, what do you want to be when you grow up? You may not have an answer right now, but have you ever dreamed of being a...

Policeman Dentist
Nurse Dancer
Truck driver
Singer
Pilot
Engineer Missionary
Teacher Plumber
Computer programmer

Do you know what it takes to become one of these? No matter what you choose, some education or training is needed.

A **career** (kuh-**reer**) is the lifework a person chooses to earn a living. Some careers require (ri-**kwī**-er) you to have more education after high school; others do not. Any education after high school is called *higher education*. Higher education can take a short time; but if you want to become a doctor, it can take as long as eight years.

To save and pay for your education, you may have many different jobs. Some jobs may not be work you enjoy. You can still make the most of them because they give you the opportunity to earn money.

These jobs are just stepping stones to take you where you want to go. Think of each job as a way to reach your career goal.

Why should you have a career goal?

A career goal will help you plan for the future. You can reach your goal if you know where you are going. For example, if you take a walk to get ice cream, you have a goal. If you just take a walk with no goal, you could miss the ice cream!

KCKs, the same thing can happen in your life if you do not set goals. You can miss the target of what God has planned for you. If you do not have any goals for the future right now, start thinking! Ask God to show you what He wants you to do. Pray for revelation of what your career goal should be. It is **The Kingdom Code** way.

Yes, it can cost a lot of time and money to reach your career goal. Where will you get the money?

START SAVING...

RIGHT NOW!

THIS MOMENT!!

NOT A MINUTE LATER!!!

 It is worth every penny you save to be happy in your career!.

Challenge!

Whatever career you choose:

- **Become the best.**
- **Seek knowledge.**
- **Trust Jesus to guide you.**

Most people do not think about what they will do after high school when they are your age, but you are a **KCK** and plan ahead.

Kingdom Code Kids Think Differently!

We save for our education now, so we can fulfill our dreams later.

To help you start thinking about a future career goal, discuss these questions.

1. What do you really like to do?

2. What skills do you have? Are you good at math, sports, building things, drawing, or computers?

3. What jobs sound like they would be fun to learn about?

4. What is interesting to you?

5. What is something you would like to try?

After sharing your ideas, name something you might want to do when you grow up. Now is a good time to set career goals. Even if you change your mind later about what career you want, you still may need some higher education to help you be a success.

?

⚜ Action Time ⚜

Let's Go
on a
Scavenger Hunt!

Divide into two or three teams. Look for items that could stand for different careers. For example, colored pencils could be for an artist. Find as many different items as you can. Tell about each item. The team who has the most items for different careers wins the game.

You know **J** is for **Jesus** and **O** is for **Others**.

Now it is time to start saving for your education. That is why the third letter in the **KCK Budget** is an **E**, because **E** stands for **Education**.

Each time you divide your money, you will put 10% into the **E Treasure Keeper**. To find this amount, multiply 0.10 times the total amount of money you are dividing into your **JOEYS Treasure Keeper**s. This is how you save for your higher education.

Total Amount of Money x 0.10 = 10% for Education

None of the money in your **Business Money Keeper** can be put into your **JOEYS** pockets.

Great Idea!

Keep your personal money separate from your business money.

Look at the circle below to see how much will be saved for education in your **KCK Budget**.

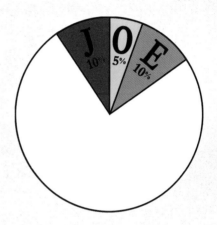

J 10% O 5% E 10%

E = 10% for *Education*

Fantastic

You found the **Clue**.

 KCKs set career goals and save ten percent of their money for education.

Code of Honor

Treasure Seeking

Diligence (**dil**-i-juns) is working with all the might and power you can give.

It means:

• Not quitting when you are really tired.

• Keeping your mind on what you are doing.

• Always trying to do your best.

Show Diligence

In your Treasure Builder, it is very important to show diligence as you work. For example, if you are pulling weeds, do not stop to talk to a friend on the phone.

Focus on your job.

Work at everything you do with all your heart. Work as if you were working for the Lord, not for human masters.

— Colossians 3:23 NIRV

Dear Kingdom Code Kids,

While I was growing up, my father and mother wanted me to learn in many different ways.

My parents always told me to use good judgment or common sense... like not getting into a car with a stranger. They taught me to take time to think about all my choices before I made a decision, and what might happen if I made the wrong choice.

School was important to my parents. They knew teachers could give me knowledge and skills I would use all my life. I attended college to prepare for the career I chose. Going to college was fun, and I got a degree too!

I went to church with Mother. We read the Bible together to understand God's wisdom and His love for me.

My parents were great mentors. They shared life stories about other people, and I learned from my parents' experiences too. Knights, I want you to listen and learn from others. Pay close attention to wise people who love you. Their advice can help you make the best decisions possible.

God bless you,
Aunt Jimmi

P.S. I hope your business is going great!

Knights, make the best decisions possible.
- Use common sense.
- Learn knowledge and skills in school.
- Read God's wisdom from the Bible.
- Listen to people's stories and experiences.

In your business...

How can you use common sense?
- Buy only supplies you need.
- Call customers if you are going to be late.

How can you use knowledge and skills you learn in school?
- Write appointments on your calendar.
- Keep your ledger up to date.

How can you use God's wisdom?
- Treat customers like you want to be treated.
- Keep your word.
- Be honest.

How can you use life experiences?
- Learn from others' successes.
- Learn from others' mistakes.

You have discovered the **Treasure**.

KCKs use common sense, knowledge, God's wisdom, and experiences to make good decisions.

1. Learn the third rule of the **KCK Sales Code**.

My KCK Sales Code

3 **I have a firm but kind handshake.**

2. Update your ledger. Make sure the amount in the **Balance** column is the same as the amount of money in your **Business Money Keeper**. If it is not the same, find the mistake and correct it. Ask for help if you cannot find your mistake.

3. Make new and follow-up sales calls if needed. Write all new appointments on your calendar.

4. Interview someone who has a career you would like to have when you grow up. Find how much education is needed for this career and what the person does every day.

Ask him or her, "What would help me prepare for this career?"

Kingdom Keys

Key to the Lesson

I will show diligence as I set goals and save money for my education.

Key Ideas

Clue to the Code
KCKs set career goals and save ten percent of their money for education.

Character Code
Show Diligence

Treasure of the Kingdom
KCKs use common sense, knowledge, God's wisdom, and experiences to make good decisions.

Key Terms

career (kuh-**reer**) the lifework a person chooses to earn a living

diligence (**dil**-i-juns) working with all the might and power you can give

I want to be a Vet, so I have to save lots of money for my education!

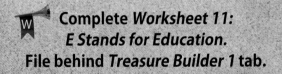

Complete *Worksheet 11: E Stands for Education.*
File behind *Treasure Builder 1* tab.

CONGRATULATIONS

You may place your Level Eleven reward on the KCK Treasure Map!

Bonus Code Work

A 1. Complete *Activity 22: Round Up Review*. When complete, file behind *Treasure Builder 1* tab.

2. Divide into teams, and pick a situation below:

- Someone knocks over a birdbath.

- You break a vase.

- A friend finds money in the classroom.

Teams should act out how they would handle their situations *with* common sense and *without* common sense. Make it a funny play or skit to show how common sense is always the best choice.

3. Make up hand motions to go with the words of the song **Kingdom Code Kids Think Differently**. Teach the song and hand motions to your friends, or perform the song for your classmates or family. You can make a music video.

4. Ask your mentor, friends, or family to share a life experience story that would help you make good decisions in your business. Write the story or draw a picture of the life experience.

Lesson 12

Y Stands for You

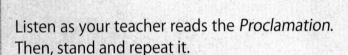

Proclamation

Listen as your teacher reads the *Proclamation*. Then, stand and repeat it.

I will do good things, so others will see what I do and praise Jesus.

You were put on this earth to bring glory to God. When you think about the needs of others by doing good deeds, spending time with others, giving gifts, or helping at home, you bring glory to Jesus.

Check Your Path

Begin *Worksheet 12: Y Stands for You.*

Quest for the Clue

Let's read about Aaron and his brother, Wyatt.

My brother and I have a small wood splitting business in Alaska, where many homes are heated by wood burning stoves. Families have to make sure they have firewood to keep their houses warm all winter long.

On Saturday, we split and stacked firewood for Mrs. Smith. It took the entire day to finish the job! We wanted to go fishing, but when we started our business, we let our customers choose when they wanted our service. Mrs. Smith chose Saturday, so we had to work on the weekend. We knew if we did not show up to work, she would have a really cold house. As we worked, I started thinking...

After all this work we've done, we should get a large pizza and buy a game to play.

Do you think Aaron and his brother took the money they made and quickly spent it on pizza and a game? Would that have been wise? If the boys had chosen to spend their money, they would have been **impulse** (**im**-puls) **buying**. Impulse buying means purchasing something without planning or thinking it through.

Guess what? Aaron and Wyatt *did not* impulse buy! They chopped wood and put their money in their **Business Money Keepers**. They chose **The Kingdom Code** way!

When you work hard and earn money, you can be proud of yourself. Rush to put your money in your **Business Money Keeper,** and watch your money grow.

Kingdom Code Kids Think Differently!

We quickly put our business money into our Business Money Keepers.

Sometimes all you can think about is how to spend your money. Be aware of thoughts that make you want to impulse buy. Your friends may say, "Get what you want! You deserve it!" TV ads and the internet have great deals that sound exciting too. Everywhere you look, there is some *thing* or *someone* trying to get you to spend your money.

⚜ Share Your Thoughts ⚜

1. What are some things people say to you that encourage you to spend money?

2. What do you see on TV, the internet, or in catalogs that would make you want to spend your money?

3. What thoughts cause you to impulse buy?

Follow The Kingdom Code pathway to make good choices.

You have found the Clue.

🔍 **KCKs spend their money wisely.**

 Complete *Activity 23: Will You Impulse Buy?* File behind *Treasure Builder 1* tab.

Code of Honor

Do you know what it means to have a good name? A person who has a good name is a person with **integrity** (in-**teg**-ri-tē). Integrity is being honest, truthful, trustworthy, and doing what is right. **The Kingdom Code** is the pathway that leads to integrity.

Develop a Good Name

When people hear your name, they should have good thoughts about you.

People should know:

- **You do what you say you will do.**

- **You can be trusted.**

- **You always tell the truth.**

- **You think of others.**

- **You do things to the best of your ability.**

A good name is to be chosen rather than great riches, loving favour rather than silver and gold.

— Proverbs 22:1 KJV

 Knights, you build a good name for yourself when you have integrity.

Treasure Seeking

Have you ever walked into a store and been tempted to impulse buy something you did not need? Later, were you glad you made the decision not to buy the item? **KCKs**, if you will stop and think before you spend your money, you will make better choices.

WHAT DO YOU REALLY NEED?

WHAT DO YOU REALLY WANT?

Challenge!

Learn to know the difference between a need and a want.

A person's **needs** should always come first. Needs are things required to help a person survive. Some needs are food and shelter. **Wants** are things a person desires but does not need to survive. Knights, it is usually not a difficult decision when buying *needs*. The hard part comes when you are choosing how to spend your money on *wants*. Be aware and guard your thoughts. Try not to get **the wants** for everything you see. Remember, when you spend money, you are a consumer. Consumers must choose carefully.

How can you choose carefully?

A good idea would be to make a list of things you want to buy. Then...

1 **Check prices at different stores.**

2 **Compare prices online.**
(*with your parent's permission*)

3 **Wait for the item to go on sale when it is out of season.**

For example, you can usually get a better price on a snowboard at the end of the season. Then you will have a new one for next year.

4 **Wait for an item's price to drop after it has been in the marketplace several months.**

For example, games and movies drop in price after they have been selling for a while.

5 **Buy used or second-hand items.**

For example, shop thrift stores, garage sales, and consignment (kun-**sīn**-munt) stores.

6 **Look at classified (klas-uh-fīd) ads in newspapers, free publications, or magazines.**

! **Remember, choose to be a wise shopper. Look for bargains (bar-gunz).**

You have learned to budget your money for *Jesus*, *Others*, and *Education*. Now, it is time for *You!* That is why the fourth letter in the **KCK Budget** is *Y*, because *Y* stands for *You*.

KCKs, the biggest part of your budget will go into your *Y Treasure Keeper*. Choosing how to spend this money may be very difficult, but it is also very exciting and rewarding. This part of the **KCK Budget** is a great responsibility.

With the money in your *Y Treasure Keeper*, you can do three things:

• **Meet your needs.**

• **Choose the things you want.**

• **Save for something that costs a lot.**

The time will come when you have money in your *Y Treasure Keeper*. When this happens, you must decide what is important enough to buy. It is your choice. You control the money.

Look at the circle below to see how much of your **KCK Budget** is for *You*.

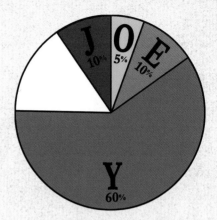

Y = 60% for You

Each time you divide your money, you will put 60% into your *Y Treasure Keeper*. To find this amount, multiply 0.60 times the total amount of money you are dividing.

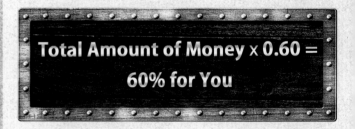

Total Amount of Money x 0.60 = 60% for You

For example, if you have $15.00 to divide into your *JOEYS* Treasure Keepers, you would multiply $15.00 times 0.60 to find 60% of your money. Your answer is $9.00, so you would put $9.00 into your *Y Treasure Keeper*.

All the money you earn from your service business must be kept in the **Business Money Keeper**. That money can only  be used to run your business. All other *Treasure Keepers* have a special purpose too, and the money in them needs to be kept for that purpose. Do not mix your money.

Let's think about another way to use your money. How can you best spend your *Y Treasure Keeper* money? **Invest** (in-**vest**) means to put money into something that could bring back a financial profit. **KCKs**, why not invest in yourself?

⚠ **One of the greatest investments you can make is to believe in yourself and start your own business!**

After Lesson 27, you will have the opportunity to invest in yourself with money from your **Business Money Keeper**. It will be quite a while before this happens, but you need to plan ahead now. Remember, 60% of everything you have in your **Business Money Keeper** will be put into your *Y Treasure Keeper* when you divide your money. It is your choice to decide how much of this money will be used to invest in yourself and a new business. Think about other businesses you might like to start. When you divide up the money after Lesson 27, the money you choose to invest in yourself will be start-up capital for your next Treasure Builder.

Did you find the **Treasure**?

KCKs are smart shoppers and use some of their money to invest in themselves.

1. Learn the next rule of the **KCK Sales Code**.

My KCK Sales Code

4 **My clothes and shoes are neat and clean so anyone is comfortable talking to me.**

2. Pick one of these four items:

Rake

Bike

Vacuum

Mop

• Find the item in three or more places.

• Compare the price, quality, and warranty of the product. (There may not be a warranty.)

• Decide the best place to buy it. Explain why. Include the sales tax and shipping charges.

3. Update your **KCK Ledger**. Then, check to make sure the amount in the **Balance** column is the same as the amount of money in your **Business Money Keeper**. If it is not the same, ask your teacher how to find the mistake. Then, correct it on your ledger.

4. Make new or follow-up sales calls if needed. Write new appointments on your calendar.

Kingdom Keys

Key to the Lesson

I will develop a good name as I build my business.

Key Ideas

Clue to the Code
KCKs spend their money wisely.

Character Code
Develop a Good Name

Treasure of the Kingdom
KCKs are smart shoppers and use some of their money to invest in themselves.

Key Terms

impulse buying (**im**-puls) (**bī**-ing) purchasing something without planning or thinking it through

invest (in-**vest**) to put money into something that could bring back a financial profit

integrity (in-**teg**-ri-tē) being honest, truthful, trustworthy, and doing what is right

needs (nēdz) things required to help a person survive

wants (wawnts) things a person desires but does not need to survive

Be a Wise Shopper.

 Complete *Worksheet 12:*
Y Stands for You.
File behind *Treasure Builder 1* tab.

CONGRATULATIONS

You may place your Level Twelve reward on the KCK Treasure Map!

Bonus Code Work

1. Choose someone who has a *good name*. Draw a picture and write a paragraph about how they show integrity.

2. Find something you think is good to invest in. Explain why it could be a good investment. Discuss this idea with your family or other students. Write what you learned.

3. Is math easy for you? Complete *Activity 24: Estimate Your Money*. File behind *Treasure Builder 1* tab.

4. Think about another Treasure Builder you might want to start. Draw a picture to show what you would be doing. Then, write two reasons it would be a good business.

5. Review Key Words from Lesson 7 through Lesson 12. Use your flash cards by yourself, with a partner, or play a game with a group. The game is played by reading the definition of a word out loud, and seeing who can shout the answer first. Keep score.

Lesson 13

S Stands for Savings

Proclamation

I will save for my future, instead of spending my money as soon as I get it.

Now, stand and repeat the *Proclamation*. What does the *Proclamation* say to do instead of impulse buying? To save for your future, practice **self-control**. Self-control means the ability to stop yourself from doing things you want to do, but might not be the best for you.

Check Your Path

 Begin *Worksheet 13: S Stands for Savings.*

Quest for the Clue

Have you ever had money *burn a hole in your pocket?*

Knights, when you have money in your pocket, sometimes all you can think about is spending it. You can hardly wait to buy something. If you feel this way, then your money is *burning a hole in your pocket.* This is when you need a plan for saving and spending your money.

Great news! After this lesson, you can use the **KCK Budget**. It will be exciting to put all your personal money into *JOEYS* Treasure Keepers.

Your KCK Budget will protect your money, so it will never *burn a hole in your pocket* again.

You have learned the first four parts of the **KCK Budget**: *Jesus*, *Others*, *Education*, and *You*. Now it is time for *Savings*. That is why the last letter in *JOEYS* is an **S**, because **S** stands for *Savings*.

When you save, you set aside money **now** so you will have it **later**. Savings gives you **security** (si-**kyoor**-i-tē). Security is the feeling of being safe.

Every time you divide your personal money, you will take 15% and put it into the *S Treasure Keeper* to save for the future. To find this amount, multiply 0.15 times the total amount of money you are dividing.

Total Amount of Money x 0.15 = 15% for Savings

This is what your **KCK Budget** now looks like with all five parts.

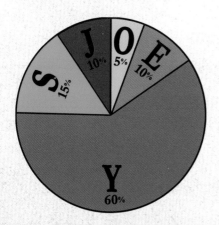

S = 15% to *Savings*

KCKs, there are two types of savings you will need. They are *Long-Term Savings* and *Emergency Savings*.

Long-Term Savings is a way to save, little by little, to buy something that costs a lot. It is for something you want in the future. For example, you may want to save for a computer, a musical instrument, a car, or a house someday. Long-Term Savings is for long-term goals. You do not want to spend it now.

Emergency Savings is the *stash* you never, ever touch until you have a true emergency! It is for things you are not expecting. For example, it can be used to pay for a lost library book or replace something you break.

Do you really need Emergency Savings?

Suppose you use all your Long-Term Savings to buy a computer, then drop the computer or spill a drink on it. With Emergency Savings, you can repair the computer. If all your savings are gone, you have no money for this disaster. Emergency Savings is the money you use for a rainy day.

How do you divide your savings? There are two ways. Pick one of these two ways to separate your savings and use it every time you divide your money into the **JOEYS** *Treasure Keepers*.

1 Take all the money in your **S** *Treasure Keeper* and make three stacks that have the same amount of money in each stack. One of the stacks is your Emergency Savings and will be put a clear, zippered pocket inside your **S** *Treasure Keeper*. The other two stacks are your Long-Term Savings.

— OR —

2 Count all the money in your **S** *Treasure Keeper* and multiple 0.30 times this amount. Your answer is your Emergency Savings and will be put in a clear, zippered pocket inside your **S** *Treasure Keeper*.

Always keep your two types of savings separate, but inside the **S** *Treasure Keeper*.

Saving is paying yourself in advance, so the money will be there when you need it. Saving can keep you from having to borrow money. It is **The Kingdom Code** way!

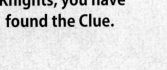

Knights, you have found the Clue.

 KCKs protect their future with Long-Term and Emergency Savings.

 Complete *Activity 25: The KCK Budget*. File behind your *Treasure Builder 1* tab.

Code of Honor

Content (kun-**tent**) means being happy with what you have.

Be Content

While Paul was in prison, he wrote to other Christians and told them he had found the secret to being content. Read the verses below to find Paul's secret.

Keep your lives free from the love of money and be content with what you have, because God has said, "Never will I leave you; never will I forsake you."

— Hebrews 13:5 NIV

I know what it's like not to have what I need. I also know what it's like to have more than I need. I have learned the secret of being content no matter what happens. I am content whether I am well fed or hungry. I am content whether I have more than enough or not enough.

— Philippians 4:12 NIRV

Paul learned that having God with him at all times was the secret to being content. Paul knew God would take care of him. It did not matter if he was poor or had great riches, Paul could be happy anywhere.

Read Hebrews 13:5 again. What can you do to be content?

Treasure Seeking

Have you ever bought something and thought it would make you happy, only to find out later it did not? Knights, having *things* does not always make you happy. *Being happy* comes from within you. It is a choice you make.

KCKs, when you look around, you find that some people have more things and money than others. It has always been this way, and it will be the same in the future. Just like all the different flavors of ice cream, people are different too.

Some are better at math, while others are better at writing or telling stories. Some people live in houses, while others live in apartments. Living in a large house does not always mean you are content. No matter where you live, what talents you have, or how much money you make, you will not be content until you _choose_ to be content.

**Kingdom Code Kids
Think Differently!**

We choose to be content.

Discuss the questions below to learn some ways to be content.

1. Name some things God has given you for which you are thankful.

2. What can happen if you depend on other people to make you happy?

3. Name some ways you can have fun without spending money.

4. Every day you see ads trying to sell you something. How can you be content when you see so many things you want?

Knights, you are learning how important it is to save money. Have you ever wondered why people save money in a pig? In the story below you learn how Eddie finds the answer.

"Dad! Dad! I mowed Mr. Baker's grass and he gave me five dollars and fifty cents!" Eddie yelled as he burst through the door. He had a smile from ear to ear across his face for getting paid for his hard work.

His father set down his tools and answered, "That's great Eddie! What are you going to do with the money?"

Eddie answered, "I don't know. What do you think I should do with it?"

His father gave him a wink, as he took off his work gloves. "You should save it in a piggy bank." Eddie's father looked around the room, walked over to a cabinet, and pulled out an orange clay jar.

"Eddie, you should keep all your money in here so you don't lose it."

Eddie looked at the jar. "That's not a piggy bank!"

His father laughed. "Yes, Eddie, you're right. It does not look like a piggy bank." Setting the jar down, Eddie's father began to explain.

"You see, years ago, people did not know how to make things out of glass or metal. Many things inside the house, like plates and cups, were made of clay."

"This clay jar and those flower pots over there are made from clay too. Long ago, the most common type of clay was found near rivers and in caves. It was called *pygg clay*."

"So what does that have to do with my money?" Eddie asked.

"Well, people have always saved money and needed somewhere to put it, so they used clay jars or pots made of pygg clay."

"Since the jars were made of pygg clay, people began calling them *pygg banks*. Later, people just started calling them *pig* or *piggy banks*."

Eddie smiled as he picked up the piggy bank and quickly stuffed his money into it. He had begun his quest to save for the future. What a great beginning!

As you save money for the future, remember the **Treasure** you found in this lesson.

Saving is easy when you are content with what you have.

1. Get ready for Lesson 14 review. Use your Key Terms flash cards and learn the Key Terms for Lessons 7 – 13. Review the words until you know them.

2. Learn rule #5 of the **KCK Sales Code**.

My KCK Sales Code

5 **I smile and say "Please" and "Thank You."**

3. Update your **KCK Ledger**. Check your **Business Money Keeper** to make sure the amount matches the balance in your ledger.

4. **If you have personal money, you can begin your budget!** Remember, none of your business money can be put into your *JOEYS* Treasure Keepers at this time. Have fun using the **KCK Budget**. You are starting a quest to manage your money wisely.

What a great beginning!

Kingdom Keys

Key to the Lesson
When I am content, I enjoy saving for my future.

Key Ideas

Clue to the Code
KCKs protect their future with Long-Term and Emergency Savings.

Character Code
Be Content

Treasure of the Kingdom
Saving is easier when you are content with what you have.

Key Terms

content (kun-**tent**) being happy with what you have

security (si-**kyoor**-i-tē) the feeling of being safe

self-control (self) (kun-**trōl**) the ability to stop yourself from doing things you want to do, but might not be the best for you

W Complete *Worksheet 13*:
   S Stands for Savings.
File behind *Treasure Builder 1* tab.

CONGRATULATIONS

You may place your Level Thirteen reward on the KCK Treasure Map.

Bonus Code Work

A 1. Make a paper mache piggy bank. Use *Activity 26: How to Make a Piggy Bank.*

A 2. Have fun with numbers. Complete *Activity 27: Whole Numbers Round Up.* File behind *Treasure Builder 1* tab.

3. Share true stories of times when *money burned a hole in your pocket.*

4. Begin a prayer journal. A journal is a notebook or papers kept together where you write thoughts and prayers. Use this journal to write letters to God. Thank Him for things that help you feel content and happy.

5. Saving money can be difficult because it takes self-control to save. Ask your family, teacher, or mentor for things they do that make it easier for them to save money.

Lesson 14

Looking Back

Proclamation

Let's review some things you have learned in Lessons 7 - 13. When you see how much you already know, your confidence will grow. You are doing a fantastic job organizing and running your business!

Stand tall and proud as you work hard to build your business.

You have learned seven *Proclamations* in Lessons 7 - 13. Use your book to review these *Proclamations*. Then, choose your favorite one.

Check Your Path

W Begin *Worksheet 14: Looking Back.*

Quest for the Clue

Do you know what it means to be in your *comfort zone*?

It means you feel happy and content while you do something. You feel secure, like a kitten drinking warm milk. Some kids are in their comfort zones when they play sports. Others are in their comfort zones when they read a book or play a game.

A few of the rules from the **KCK Sales Code** may take you *out* of your comfort zone. That is OK. Just like a turtle has to come out of its shell, sometimes you do too! It may be difficult, but every rule of the code is important to learn and practice as you make sales calls.

Let's review the KCK Sales Code. Read each rule out loud.

My KCK Sales Code

1. My hair, hands, body, and teeth are clean.

2. I look into the other person's eyes when we talk to each other.

3. I have a firm but kind handshake.

4. My clothes and shoes are neat and clean so anyone is comfortable talking to me.

5. I smile and say, "Please" and "Thank You."

6. I listen carefully and do not interrupt.

7. I speak slowly, clearly, and loudly enough so people will understand me.

8. I only make promises I can keep.

9. I take an adult with me when I make face-to-face sales calls.

10. I ask God to help me find favor with everyone I meet.

The KCK Sales Code helps me make a great first impression!

With God's help, I will look great and act amazing.

My KCK Sales Code

The Kingdom Code

Share Your Thoughts

Step *out* of your comfort zones for a minute. Use the **KCK Sales Code** to discuss the questions below:

1. Which rule helps you the most in sales?

2. Which rules are the easiest for you, and why?

3. Which rules are the most difficult, and why?

4. If others talk about a rule that is easy for them but not for you, learn how they do it. Do not be afraid to ask for help!

5. If there is a rule that is easy for you, but difficult for others, share your ideas and try to help others be successful.

Kingdom Code Kids Think Differently!

We have the courage to ask for help.

You have found the Clue.

KCKs follow a code and help each other succeed!

Knights, you are known by the things you choose to do and talk about. Always try to make a great first impression because you may have only one chance to build a good **reputation** (rep-yu-**tā**-shun). A reputation is what others believe or think about another person. For example, if you are upset and angry with someone, try very hard to use soft, kind words to express how you feel. What you say and do is the way others will remember you.

Build a Good Reputation

Let's read what Jesus did when He was twelve years old.

After three days they found him in the temple courtyard. He was sitting with the teachers. He was listening to them and asking them questions. Everyone who heard him was amazed at how much he understood. They also were amazed at his answers.

— Luke 2:46-47 NIRV

When Jesus traveled to Jerusalem with His parents, He went into the temple where He listened to the teachers and asked questions. He made a good first impression. In fact, Jesus was finding favor with God and man as He studied with the priests and rabbis (**rab**-īs).

Jesus was building a good reputation, even when He was young. So can you. Remember, people are always watching what you do and listening to what you say. God sees you too. Make God happy with your actions and words. It is **The Kingdom Code** way!

Treasure Seeking

When you read about people who lived in another century or even fifty years before you, some of the details of their lives may not be known. You can only guess what they did or how they dressed on a certain day.

Historical fiction (hi-**stor**-i-kul) (**fik**-shun) describes imaginary stories about facts, events, or people from the past. Authors often use historical fiction to make the past more interesting and exciting. Their stories include facts about the times when the stories took place, but also contain information that *may* or *may not* have happened. Let's read an example of historical fiction.

✦– Historical Fiction –✦

"Buy some squash, sir?" Henry looked up at the man passing by on the street. "I also have fresh tomatoes."

The man looked at this eight-year-old boy holding his basket of vegetables. "Son, I'd like some of those onions... how much?"

In this way, Henry J. Heinz started the Heinz Company, which is famous for its ketchup. Now, you may ask, "What does selling vegetables have to do with ketchup?" Let's find out!

Henry Heinz started his business at eight years of age selling extra vegetables from his mother's garden. Soon, he realized his neighbors would pay him to deliver vegetables to their homes. He was able to make a profit by buying vegetables from the farmers' markets and selling them to his neighbors.

By the time he graduated from high school, he was running a very successful business by simply buying and reselling vegetables.

After high school, Mr. Heinz began canning horseradish to sell to his vegetable customers. Horseradish is a white, very spicy sauce made from grating the root of a horseradish plant. It can be used on roast beef. It is also found in shrimp cocktail sauce. Horseradish is so strong, it can make your eyes water when you eat it.

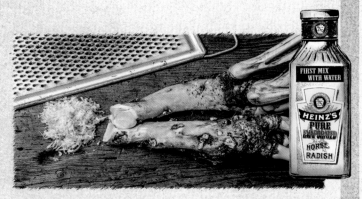

Now, Mr. Heinz would often say, "To do a common thing uncommonly well brings success." This means that to be successful, you have to be better than others at what you do. Henry practiced this belief even when he first sold vegetables.

At the time Henry began canning, everyone canned horseradish in green jars, but not Henry! He canned his in clear jars. Why? While selling vegetables, he discovered how much people cared about the quality of the products they were buying.

He came up with the clever idea of putting his horseradish in clear jars, so his customers could see what they were buying. Providing a quality product and running an honest business paved the way for the modern H. J. Heinz Company. At the same time, Mr. Heinz was building quite a reputation.

After several years of canning and selling horseradish, Mr. Heinz left his vegetable business and joined with his brother and a friend to add pickles, vinegar, and ketchup to his horseradish business. The good quality of their products allowed them to make a very nice profit. Henry's honesty and ability to think of new ideas and new ways of doing things was the pathway leading to a very successful business.

Today, the Heinz Company produces more than 5,000 products and has thousands of employees. Yet it all started with a young boy who sold and delivered vegetables to his neighbors. Henry built his business on two of his talents. He used **creativity** (krē-ā-**tiv**-i-tē). Creativity is making new things or coming up with new ideas. For example, he thought of delivering vegetables to customers. He also had **determination** (di-tur-muh-**nā**-shun). Determination means not giving up. Mr. Heinz worked very hard to be the best at what he did, and he succeeded.

SUCCESS DOES NOT JUST HAPPEN.

YOU MAKE IT HAPPEN!

KCKs, SUCCESS IS BUILT!

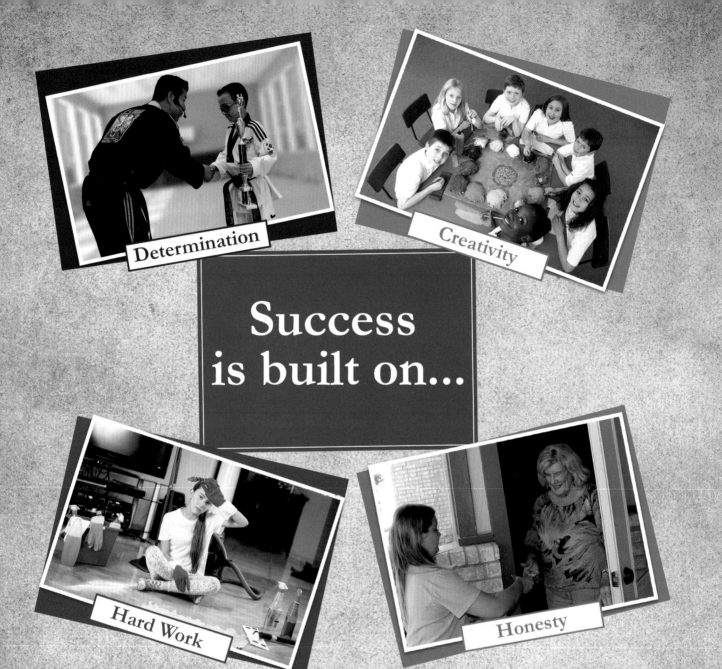

Success is built on...

Determination

Creativity

Hard Work

Honesty

You have found the **Treasure**.

KCKs are creative, honest, and show determination as they grow their businesses.

On Your Own

1. A successful business is built on money management, so keep your **KCK Ledger** up to date. *You will use your up-to-date ledger in Lesson 15.*

2. Make follow-up sales calls to customers who need to schedule appointments. Fill in the *Follow-up Report* on the back of each *Customer Sales Form* every time you contact a customer.

Kingdom Keys

Key to the Lesson

I can build a good reputation if I look great, work hard, and do all things well.

Key Ideas

Clue to the Code
KCKs follow a code and help each other succeed!

Character Code
Build a Good Reputation

Treasure of the Kingdom
KCKs are creative, honest, and show determination as they grow their businesses.

Key Terms

creativity (krē-ā-**tiv**-i-tē) making new things or coming up with new ideas

determination (di-tur-muh-**nā**-shun) not giving up

historical fiction (hi-**stor**-i-kul) (**fik**-shun) imaginary stories about facts, events, or people from the past

reputation (rep-yū-**tā**-shun) what others believe and think about another person

Ⓦ Complete *Worksheet 14: Looking Back.*
File behind *Treasure Builder 1* tab.

Success is built on...
creativity,
determination,
hard work,
and honesty!

CONGRATULATIONS

You may place your Level Fourteen reward on the KCK Treasure Map.

Bonus Code Work

1. Prepare a meal using horseradish. Tell the story about Mr. Heinz as you serve the meal.

2. What things must you do to build your business that take you *out* of your comfort zone? For example, do you find it difficult to make sales calls, ask for payment, write a thank you note, or update your ledger? Ask your mentor or family for ideas that would help make it easier. Make a poster, and draw what takes you *out* of your comfort zone in the middle of the poster. Then, around this idea, draw or paste pictures showing positive ideas that could help you.

3. Either by yourself or with your classmates, create a jingle to help you remember what the letters *JOEYS* stand for in your **KCK Budget**. You could sing, write a poem, or create a video.

4. Have a class ketchup contest. Bring several different brands of ketchup to class to sample. Take a survey to find the favorite one. Be sure to blindfold the tasters.

5. Research an entrepreneur from the past who started a successful business. Write a story that is historical fiction about this person. Share your story.

Lesson 15

Time for a Check Up

Proclamation

Read and repeat the *Proclamation*.

I will try new things and test new ideas, so I can choose what works best for me!

Knights, all your life you will have many opportunities to *try* new things. You will also be given the chance to *think about* different ways of doing things. When this happens, ask God to help you make the best choice for your life. Pray for Him to guide you so you will always make the right decision.

Check Your Path

Begin *Worksheet 15: Time for a Check Up.*

Quest for the Clue

There are special machines that doctors use so they can quickly **evaluate** (ih-**val**-yū-āt) or carefully judge the value or condition of something. For example, an X-ray machine is used to take pictures of your bones. Other machines are used to look inside you and take pictures of your organs.

With the pictures from these machines, a doctor can spot areas in your body that are OK and areas that need help. After looking at the test results (ri-**zults**), the doctor can evaluate your problem and decide how to treat you.

It is time for a check up, but there is no need to call the doctor. You are about to evaluate your service business. Why? You need to look at the Business Plan you wrote in Lesson 4 to decide what **is** or **is not** working. **KCKs**, you need to know if your business is meeting the goals you set. When you ask yourself questions, and take the time to think about all the possible answers, you are making an evaluation (ih-val-yū-**ā**-shun). The time has come to do it.

KCKs, evaluate your business like a doctor evaluates a patient (**pā**-shunt). When you go to the doctor, you are asked, "What is wrong?" In your Business Evaluation, you ask yourself, "Is there anything I need to improve?"

The doctor runs tests and looks at test results; you will carefully look at your Business Plan.

The doctor decides how to make you feel better; you will decide what changes can be made to improve your business. The doctor may research and seek advice from others; you may do the same.

Let's evaluate!

On your mark!
Get set!
Charge!

In your evaluation, you look at your Business Plan, answer questions, and make evaluations. You will also write a **summary** (**sum**-uh-rē). A summary is a short review giving the main points of something.

The summary is the most important step in your business evaluation. If you find any problems, the summary is where you write your **solutions** (suh-**loo**-shunz). Solutions are answers to problems. This is also where you talk about the future of your company.

You have found the **Clue**.

KCKs evaluate their businesses, look for problems, and find solutions.

Begin *Activity 28: Business Evaluation*. You will use *Activity 4: Business Plan* (behind *Treasure Builder 1* tab) to complete *Activity 28.* Place both activities behind *Current Work* tab until complete.

Code of Honor

And let us not grow weary of doing good, for in due season we will reap, if we do not give up.

— Galatians 6:9 ESV

The spiritual person judges all things...

— 1 Corinthians 2:15a ESV

Knights, do not give up when you are trying to reach a goal. Be **expectant** (ik-**spek**-tunt). Expectant is to believe or act like something good is going to happen. When you are expectant, you believe the future is going to be amazing. It may not be easy. It may take longer to get what you want, but you must keep trying and have a good attitude. That is **The Kingdom Code** way.

Be Expectant

To be successful, it takes a lot of hard work, determination, creativity, and honesty. For your Treasure Builder to succeed, you must be aware of what is going on in every area of your business. As you evaluate your service business, do not get discouraged if things are not going as planned. Be expectant. Have faith that things will turn out fine. Remember to look at the good things about your business, and correct what needs to be changed.

 Everyone has problems, but winners find solutions.

✦ Action Time ✦

Divide into groups of three or four students. Think of an event when you would be expectant. Show something that could go wrong. Pretend one person has a good attitude when things go wrong, while another student does not have a good attitude and is not expectant. Act out the event.

For example, pretend there is going to be a surprise birthday party for your dad. Your mother calls to say she has run out of gas while returning with the cake. Show what might happen, but let your event have a happy ending. Be creative and have fun.

✦ Historical Fiction ✦

The following story about Thomas Edison is historical fiction. Let's read what *might have* happened in Mr. Edison's lab. Knights, enjoy learning about the man who once said:

"I have not failed. I've just found 10,000 ways that won't work."

Thomas Alva Edison.

It was three 'o clock in the morning, and Mr. Edison gently laid his head down on his desk. He was worn out! He and his team had been working on the same problem for months, but had not been able to find the right type of material that would work. It had to stand up to an electric current being forced through it, and also had to glow brightly enough to light up a room.

You see, Mr. Edison and his team were trying to invent the electric light bulb. They had experimented for a very long time, but all the materials they tried had failed.

Turning his head to stare at the flickering oil lamp, Mr. Edison was sure there was a way to put electricity in every home instead of oil. He had faith in his team and knew they would overcome this problem.

It was at that moment he heard a knock at the door. "Come in," Mr. Edison said. The door opened slowly, and before him stood David. David was the quiet sort, yet he was superb when it came to problem solving and new ideas. This was the very reason Mr. Edison had him on the team.

"Sir, experiment one thousand and one just failed. The bulb exploded after twenty seconds. The filament that the electricity traveled through just could not handle the current."

Putting on his best smile, Mr. Edison decided to share a truth with David that he held very near to his heart. "Son, don't get so discouraged. We have not failed; we have successfully learned something that does not work. Be expectant!"

David gave him a puzzled look, so Mr. Edison explained. "We have learned one thousand and one things that do **not** make a light bulb. Now we don't have to worry about trying them again. You see, it's not about simply learning what works, but we have to make sure it is the best. To do that, we have to try thousands of times to find the best possible solution."

While he was talking, Mr. Edison had been fiddling with the button on his sweater and was now rubbing between his fingers a piece of thread that had come loose.

Smiling at Mr. Edison, David said, "Thank you, sir. We will try again, and we will succeed... even if it takes another thousand tries!"

"That's the spirit, son!" Mr. Edison gave him a friendly pat on the back. Then, in a sudden moment of clear thinking, Mr. Edison looked down at the loose thread from his button that he held in his hand. "David, have we tried thread yet?"

"Thread, sir?" David looked confused.

"Yes! Thread!" Running into the lab, Mr. Edison took the thread in his hand and carefully formed it into a filament. Calling for a bulb, he put it all together and placed it in the electrical socket. The light bulb glowed brightly for almost fourteen hours!

That may not sound like a long time to you and me, but for Mr. Edison and his team, it was almost fourteen hours longer than anything else they had tried.

In order to be successful, Mr. Edison kept working and expecting to find the best possible answer. Even though it took him and his team thousands of tries before they met success, they never quit. They never gave up!

Did you turn on the lights in your room this morning? That proves you should never give up on a great idea. God has big plans for you and your ideas too.

Kingdom Code Kids Think Differently!

We evaluate our lives and make corrections when things are not working.

KCKs, you evaluate things every day. Have you ever asked yourself:

- **Do my new shoes hurt my feet?**

- **Which candy bar do I want to buy?**

- **Am I too sick to go to school?**

- **Do I want to learn how to play a guitar?**

- **Should I start a new business or keep doing the one I have now?**

Treasure Seeking

Knights, have the courage to evaluate things around you. Be brave. Look at areas in your life that might need help. For example, if you cannot read well, multiply quickly, hit a baseball, or make new friends easily, think of ways you can improve. You might make some changes, or try something new to get what you want. Have faith; God will help you.

Trying new things and testing new ideas can turn out great, but sometimes they do not. Things usually turn out best if you take time to evaluate before making a decision.

You have found the **Treasure**.

KCKs evaluate things in their lives so they can make the best decisions.

❧ Share Your Thoughts ☙

1. Discuss the following people in the Bible. Look at the choices they made. *Why* did they make these choices? Do you think they evaluated their situations?

   • Zacchaeus climbed a tree. (Luke 19:1-10)

   • Jonah ran away on a ship. (Jonah 1)

   • From the rooftop, men lowered their friend down into a room. (Luke 5:17-26)

2. If someone wants you to try something new, what questions should you ask yourself to help make your decision?

3. When things are not going right or you think an idea is not a good one, describe at least two feelings you have.

4. Why should you evaluate?

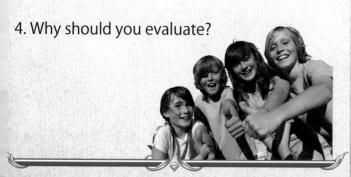

1. Complete *Activity 28: Business Evaluation* using *Activity 4: Business Plan*. File *Activity 4* behind *Treasure Builder 1* tab when you finish using it.

2. When *Activity 28: Business Evaluation* is complete, take it home and discuss ways to improve your business with your family. Bring *Activity 28* back to class, and file behind *Treasure Builder 1* tab.

3. Learn rule #6 of the **KCK Sales Code**. Say it until you know it.

My KCK Sales Code

6 **I listen carefully and do not interrupt.**

Kingdom Keys

Key to the Lesson

If I am expectant, I can evaluate, find solutions, and improve things in my life.

Key Ideas

Clue to the Code
KCKs evaluate their businesses, look for problems, and find solutions.

Character Code
Be Expectant

Treasure of the Kingdom
KCKs evaluate things in their lives so they can make the best decisions.

Key Terms

evaluate (ih-**val**-yū-āt) carefully judge the value or condition of something

expectant (ik-**spek**-tunt) to believe or act like something good is going to happen

solution (suh-**loo**-shun) an answer to a problem

summary (**sum**-uh-rē) a short review giving the main points of something

Be Expectant!

Complete *Worksheet 15:*
Time for a Check Up.
File behind *Treasure Builder 1* tab.

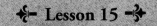

CONGRATULATIONS

You may place your Level Fifteen reward on the KCK Treasure Map!

Bonus Code Work

1. Ask your friends how their businesses are going. Then, have a "business meeting" to discuss any problems or successes any of you are having. This is a great time to work as a team and help each other.

2. Write historical fiction about a person or an event from the past. Include some facts and some fiction in your story. You can put yourself in the story as one of the characters.

3. Look all around your room to evaluate if anything needs to be repaired or given away. Take action! Then, write about what you did.

4. Use your flash cards to practice your Key Terms. You may practice with a friend.

Kingdom Code Kids are Great Leaders and Entrepreneurs. We...

- Follow the **KCK Sales Code**.
- Trust God to guide us.
- Know what is happening in our businesses.
- Work hard to be the best at what we do.
- Manage our money well.
- Treat others like we want to be treated.

KCKs

KCKs choose to be outstanding Knights in God's Army!

Army of God

Lesson 16

Arthur's Armor Repair

Proclamation

Instead of talking about making money, I will work hard to earn it.

Stand and say the *Proclamation* out loud. While you are standing, put on the Armor of God.

In this lesson you will meet Arthur, and read about how he works hard to earn money in his armor repair business.

Check Your Path

Begin *Worksheet 16: Arthur's Armor Repair.*

Quest for the Clue

Hi, my name is Arthur and I live in a great, walled city. In January, I became the owner of Arthur's Armor Repair, which is the blacksmith business that has been in my family for as long as I can remember. The business came with tools, a workshop, and lots of customers.

The King even uses my business to polish his armor and make repairs. People all over the kingdom know our advertisement.

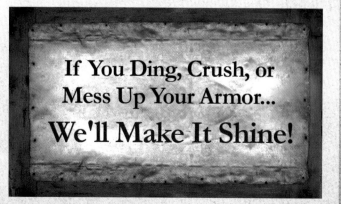

If You Ding, Crush, or Mess Up Your Armor...
We'll Make It Shine!

Lesson 16

Arthur's Armor Repair

Proclamation

Instead of talking about making money, I will work hard to earn it.

Stand and say the *Proclamation* out loud. While you are standing, put on the Armor of God.

In this lesson you will meet Arthur, and read about how he works hard to earn money in his armor repair business.

Quest for the Clue

Hi, my name is Arthur and I live in a great, walled city. In January, I became the owner of Arthur's Armor Repair, which is the blacksmith business that has been in my family for as long as I can remember. The business came with tools, a workshop, and lots of customers.

The King even uses my business to polish his armor and make repairs. People all over the kingdom know our advertisement.

Check Your Path

Begin *Worksheet 16: Arthur's Armor Repair.*

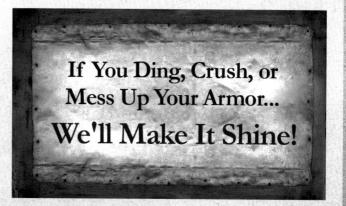

If You Ding, Crush, or Mess Up Your Armor... We'll Make It Shine!

When I took over in January, our business was booming. The knights had just returned from a jousting match where they tested their skills against knights from far and wide. There was plenty of repair work to be done! At the end of the month, my bills were all paid and my business was doing great.

I am very careful to keep my ledger up to date. I would like to show it to you now. Before I do, you need to know about two types of business expenses. See the chart below.

Two Types of Business Expenses:

A **fixed expense** is a business cost which usually does not change. These expenses stay the same week after week.

Arthur's fixed expenses:
- Salary (**sal**-uh-rē)
- Employee salary
- Snacks

A **variable** (**vair**-ē-uh-bul) **expense** is a business cost which can change. These expenses can be different amounts each week.

Arthur's variable expenses:
- Metal polish
- Wood
- Candles

Fixed Expenses + Variable Expenses = Total Expenses

KCKs, let's look at Arthur's ledger on the next page. First look for Arthur's salary, which is a *fixed expense*. Is his salary the same amount of money all four weeks? When something happens again and again, it is called a *pattern*.

Now, let's find a *variable expense*. Look for how much Arthur paid for wood. Do the wood purchases cost the same amount every week? When expenses do not stay the same, they change, or **vary** (**vair**-ē). That is why they are called *variable expenses*.

Arthur's Armor Repair Ledger

Date	Description	Income	Expenses	Balance
1/1	Beginning Balance			$1,000.00
1/3	Arthur – salary		125.00	875.00
1/3	Betty's Bakery – snacks		5.00	870.00
1/3	King Daniel – repair 10 sets of armor	400.00		1,270.00
1/4	Metal Polish – purchase		20.00	1,250.00
1/4	Wood – purchase		10.00	1,240.00
1/6	Candles – purchase		5.00	1,235.00
1/6	Sir William – armor repair	75.00		1,310.00
1/7	Advertising (business cards)		5.00	1,305.00
1/8	Tony – employee salary		50.00	1,255.00
	Weekly balance			$1,255.00
1/10	Arthur – salary		125.00	1,130.00
1/10	Betty's Bakery – snacks		5.00	1,125.00
1/10	Sir John – polish armor (family collection)	275.00		1,400.00
1/11	Metal Polish – purchase		25.00	1,375.00
1/11	Wood – purchase		15.00	1,360.00
1/12	Sir Scott – helmet repair	73.00		1,433.00
1/13	Candles – purchase		3.00	1,430.00
1/14	Advertising (posters and flyers)		7.00	1,423.00
1/15	Tony – employee salary		50.00	1,373.00
	Weekly balance			$1,373.00
1/17	Arthur – salary		125.00	1,248.00
1/17	Betty's Bakery – snacks		5.00	1,243.00
1/17	Sir William – polish armor	81.00		1,324.00
1/18	Metal Polish – purchase		26.00	1,298.00
1/18	Wood – purchase		11.00	1,287.00
1/19	Candles – purchase		4.00	1,283.00
1/20	Advertising (flyers)		3.00	1,280.00
1/21	Duke Larry – lance repair (jousting team)	250.00		1,530.00
1/22	Tony – employee salary		50.00	1,480.00
	Weekly balance			$1,480.00
1/23	Arthur – salary		125.00	1,355.00
1/23	Betty's Bakery – snacks		5.00	1,350.00
1/24	Metal Polish – purchase		23.00	1,327.00
1/24	Wood – purchase		9.00	1,318.00
1/25	Candles – purchase		3.00	1,315.00
1/26	Advertising (flyers)		3.00	1,312.00
1/27	Duke Larry – polish shields (jousting team)	175.00		
1/28	Tony – employee salary		50.00	
1/28	Squire Jerry – refit armor	100.00		
1/31	Ending Balance			$1,537.00

Anytime you operate a business, it is important to do everything you can to make it a success. This takes **initiative** (ih-**nish**-uh-tiv). Initiative is knowing what needs to be done and doing it. Knights, think about your customers and what they might need. Take initiative by looking for something extra you can do for them. It will make your customers happy.

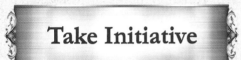
Take Initiative

Arthur works in his shop almost every day. He knows what is happening in his business. He does not just talk about keeping his ledger up to date; he does it. By writing every transaction in his ledger, Arthur always knows his income and expenses. If his business is ever in trouble, he will see it right away.

No matter what you do, work at it with all your might...

— Ecclesiastes 9:10a NIRV

When you take initiative, you work with a happy heart and try to do more than what is expected. This pleases God and others.

This **Clue** is very important.

🔍 **KCKs keep their ledgers up to date, so they know how their businesses are doing.**

📯 Complete *Activity 29: Arthur's Armor Repair Ledger.* File behind *Treasure Builder 1* tab.

Kingdom Code Kids Think Differently!

We take initiative by doing more than what is expected.

KCKs do not just *get by;* they go the extra mile. That is **The Kingdom Code** way!

Four Ways to Take Initiative

When I see someone in need, I jump in and help.

Example: When you see an older person going toward a door, walk over and open the door.

When I see a job that needs to be done, I do it without being asked.

Example: If you see a dirty counter, take a minute to clean it.

When I have a job to do, I look for ways to do something more than is expected.

Example: When you set the table, make sure every place has a napkin. You can even fold it in a fancy way.

I do not put off until tomorrow, the things I can do today.

Example: If you have a project, finish it right away instead of waiting until the last minute.

⚜ Action Time ⚜

Take Initiative!

Divide into teams for skits.

Act out one of the four ways to take initiative or choose another way to show initiative. Try to guess what the other teams are acting out.

Take initiative every day.

Treasure Seeking

Three months have passed for Arthur at Arthur's Armor Repair. The last time he looked at his ledger, something was terribly wrong.

What could it be?
What has changed?

- Knights still wear armor.

- Armor still needs to be repaired and polished.

- Several jousting matches have taken place, but Arthur's shop has received very little business.

Arthur is worried!

Arthur needs to find what is wrong, so he decides to use his **Income Statements** and make graphs to study his business.

Using his **Income Statements**, Arthur finds the difference between his **Total Income** and his **Total Expenses.** This shows the **Profit** or **Loss** for each month. *Oh, no!* Arthur realizes his income went down every month.

This is not a good **trend**. A trend is a direction something moves or changes. His income has gone *down*, not *up*. Arthur has a big problem and needs a solution. Knights, Arthur needs your help!

To solve his problem, Arthur has collected his **data** (dā-tuh). Data are facts or information, usually used to study or plan something. Below are Arthur's **Income Statements** for the last four months showing the data he gathered.

January Income Statement	
Total Income	**$1409.00**
Fixed Expenses	$520.00
Variable Expenses	$352.00
Total Expenses	**$872.00**
Profit or **Loss**	**$537.00**

February Income Statement	
Total Income	**$1273.00**
Fixed Expenses	$520.00
Variable Expenses	$325.00
Total Expenses	**$845.00**
Profit or **Loss**	**$428.00**

March Income Statement	
Total Income	**$834.00**
Fixed Expenses	$520.00
Variable Expenses	$263.00
Total Expenses	**$783.00**
Profit or **Loss**	**$51.00**

April Income Statement	
Total Income	**$521.00**
Fixed Expenses	$520.00
Variable Expenses	$275.00
Total Expenses	**$795.00**
Profit or **Loss**	**($274.00)**

This bar graph below shows Arthur's income and expenses for January, February, March, and April. The **blue bar** shows **Income** and the **red bar** shows **Expenses** for each month.

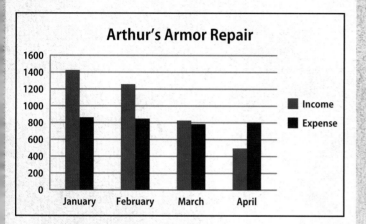

Arthur's Armor Repair

This line graph below shows the same data in a different way.

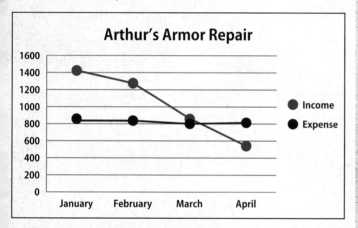

Arthur's Armor Repair

The data in the charts and graphs are for you to **analyze** (**an**-uh-līz). Analyze means to study something carefully. **KCKs**, your quest is to analyze the data.

Use your book to complete *Activity 30: Analyze Arthur's Data*. File behind *Treasure Builder 1* tab.

You have analyzed the data from the charts and graphs. Now, your quest is to take this information and help Arthur find a solution.

What You Know...

The data shows Arthur had less income every month, with a very large income loss in March.

By looking for changes in Income, Expenses, and Profit each month, you quickly know how a company is doing.

Maybe you should ask Arthur if he remembers what changed from February to March.

What You Find...

When you talk to Arthur, you make a discovery. He tells you he tried to save money and bought a very low-priced armor polish. He began using it the end of February, but realized the armor was not as shiny as before. He bought too much of the polish to throw it away, so he hoped no one would notice the difference.

More Data You Uncover...

In March, the King's knights did not bring him any work. He did not understand, because there had been a jousting match in February.

Arthur began to panic. He did not know what he should do!

To cut back on expenses, Arthur made the decision to stop advertising. He had no work for two days, so he took off the rest of the week to go fishing. While fishing, he came up with an idea. He decided to raise his prices. He believed this would help him earn back the money he lost.

When a customer did not think the higher price was fair, Arthur got angry and yelled at him. Nothing was working!

Challenge!

Can you form a plan to help Arthur save his business?

⚔ Share Your Thoughts ⚔

What do you think Arthur could do to solve his problem?

Find Solutions for Arthur:

1. Should Arthur keep using the bargain armor polish?

2. Should he start advertising again?

3. Should he change his prices?

4. Name some things that Arthur could do for the unhappy customer.

5. How can he get the King's business back?

6. Are there any expenses he could cut until he gets his business going again?

7. How could he get more customers?

Discuss the Solutions:

• Knights, do your ideas make sense?

• Which ideas should Arthur put into action?

• Is it possible to put them into action?

• Why do you think your strategy will work?

KCKs, do you realize what you have just done? You have created a **Problem Solving Plan** to help Arthur. You can use this plan to solve problems in your own business too.

Let's review the six steps of your Problem Solving Plan.

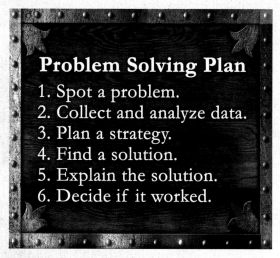

Problem Solving Plan

1. Spot a problem.
2. Collect and analyze data.
3. Plan a strategy.
4. Find a solution.
5. Explain the solution.
6. Decide if it worked.

Reminder!

Knights, sometimes your ideas to fix a problem will not work. What should you do?

You can pray for wisdom, review the Problem Solving Plan, and talk to your family or mentor.

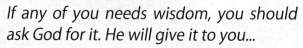

If any of you needs wisdom, you should ask God for it. He will give it to you...
— James 1:5a NIRV

Always try to stay positive and have a good attitude. There is nothing too big that you cannot face and conquer with God's help. He is always with you to give comfort and strength when you struggle with a problem. If you ask, He will give you wisdom.

Guess what? Arthur had a *fantastic* month in May! You used the **Problem Solving Plan**, and your ideas worked. Way to go, **KCKs**!

Knights, you have found the Treasure.

KCKs solve problems by analyzing data, forming a plan, and putting the plan into action!

On Your Own

1. Update your ledger. Make sure every transaction is entered. Be sure the amount of money in your **Business Money Keeper** matches your ending balance in your ledger.

2. Learn rule #7 of the **KCK Sales Code**. Say it until you know it.

My KCK Sales Code

7 I speak slowly, clearly, and loudly so people will understand me.

Kingdom Keys

Key to the Lesson
I take initiative by keeping an up-to-date ledger and solving problems quickly!

Key Ideas

Clue to the Code
KCKs keep their ledgers up to date, so they know how their businesses are doing.

Character Code
Take Initiative

Treasure of the Kingdom
KCKs solve problems by analyzing data, forming a plan, and putting the plan into action!

Key Terms

analyze (**an**-uh-līz) to study something carefully

data (**dā**-tuh) facts or information, usually used to study or plan something

fixed expense (fikst) (ik-**spens**) a business cost which usually does not change

initiative (ih-**nish**-uh-tiv) knowing what needs to be done and doing it

trend (trind) a direction something moves or changes

variable expense (**vair**-ē-uh-bul) (ik-**spens**) a business cost which can change

**Complete *Worksheet 16: Arthur's Armor Repair*.
File behind *Treasure Builder 1* tab.**

CONGRATULATIONS

You may place your Level Sixteen reward on your KCK Treasure Map.

Bonus Code Work

1. Read a mystery novel and write a book report. In the report, tell how the **Problem Solving Plan** helped solve the mystery.

2. Play a game with some friends. Put your Key Term flash cards in a pile on a table. Each person picks four Key Terms and must make up a question that would have the Key Term as the answer. For example, the person would ask "What is the answer to a problem called?" The person who slaps his hand on the table first gets to answer, "Solution." If the person is correct, he gets a point and asks the next question. Keep score, and see who becomes the **KCK** Key Terms *King* or *Queen*.

3. Make a list of all your customers. Beside each name, write something extra you can do to take initiative the next time you help that customer.

4. Create a bar graph or a line graph using data from your ledger. Make sure your ledger is up to date before you begin. Look at the graph with your mentor and discuss what it shows.

Lesson 17

Discover Your Gifts

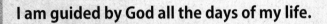

Proclamation

I am guided by God all the days of my life.

Now, stand and repeat the *Proclamation*.

How does God guide you? The Bible helps you know what to say and do by giving you **principles** (**prin**-suh-pulz). Principles are rules and beliefs which guide your thoughts, words, and actions. If you live by God's principles, you are blessed with favor, joy, and contentment.

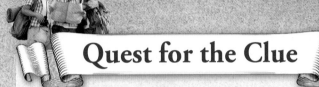

Quest for the Clue

KCKs, did you know everything you **do** has a **consequence** (**kon**-si-kwens)? A consequence is something that happens because of an action. Every **choice** you make has a consequence too. For example, if you choose to eat too much candy, the consequence could be that you get sick. On the other hand, if you eat a small amount of candy, you can enjoy it and usually not get sick.

When there is a choice to be made and you cannot make up your mind, think about what the consequences could be. You will always make a better decision if you consider all that might happen.

Kingdom Code Kids Think Differently!

We know every choice we make has a consequence.

Check Your Path

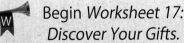

Begin *Worksheet 17: Discover Your Gifts.*

What do you dream about doing someday? Let's read a letter from Aunt Jimmi to find how she used her talent to build her first business.

From: Aunt Jimmi

Dear Kingdom Code Kids,

When I was a child, I visited my Aunt Lottie. She was an artist. I watched as she brushed the beautiful colors on her canvas. Oh, how I wanted to paint, but I was not brave enough to tell her. Knights, fear can keep you from discovering and using your God-given talents. God wants you to be bold!

Many years later, I married Johnny and finally told him my secret wish to paint. He gave me a paint set, and I tried to paint roses. By accident, I mixed the pink with the blue and made purple roses. I was upset! Johnny put his arm around me and encouraged me to take art lessons. I did, and many art teachers became my mentors. The more I learned, the more I wanted to have an art career. Did you know education is needed for almost anything you want to do?

I painted and took lessons almost three years before I sold my first painting. I made lots of mistakes, and many pictures were thrown away. Even when it was hard, I just kept trying to get better. I loved what I was doing, and each sale made me more confident.

My Aunt Lottie did not know it, but she planted a seed of desire in my heart when I was very young. She introduced

me to the beauty of color. My desire to paint eventually turned into my first Treasure Builder. Sometimes my paintings sold quickly; sometimes not. I didn't realize it, but I was learning to be an entrepreneur while I was having fun.

Do you have a secret wish? Be bold, and try to make your wish come true. If God can help me become an artist, He can surely give you the courage to follow your dreams too!

May God bless you,
Aunt Jimmi

Did you find the **Clue**?

To have a fun career, KCKs follow their dreams and develop their gifts.

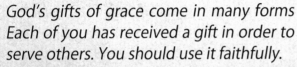
Become Confident

God's gifts of grace come in many forms Each of you has received a gift in order to serve others. You should use it faithfully.

— 1 Peter 4:10 NIRV

In this verse, Peter was talking about a **spiritual** (**spir**-i-choo-ul) **gift**, which is a special ability given by God. Examples of spiritual gifts are teaching, serving, being a leader, and sharing with others. Spiritual gifts are given to you so you can help spread the news of Jesus and help other Christians become stronger and wiser. This is one kind of gift from God.

Your talent is another kind of gift from God. It may take many years to become confident enough to develop that talent. If you are a super chess player, violinist, or softball player, you may already know what your talent is. Find and use your gifts from God to help others. Be confident as you use them.

Do you think God would have created you and not given you a special talent? No way! God does amazing work. He gave you talents and spiritual gifts. Wow! You have been given a double dose of God's grace.

Can you use your talents and leave God out? Yes. Some athletes, actors, musicians, authors, and leaders of countries, who are known all over the world, have amazing skills and talents. Many of them choose to use their talents to glorify God and help people, while others use their gifts just for money, power, or selfish reasons. **Knights, it is a choice!**

Choose to let the whole world see Christ's light shining through your spiritual gifts and talents.

Complete *Activity 31: Exploring My Talents.*

✥ Share Your Thoughts ✥

1. What special talents and gifts do you see in each other?

2. Using talents with spiritual gifts helps others see Jesus. Give examples of how talents can be used with:

   • Being a Leader.
   • Sharing with Others.
   • Teaching.
   • Serving Others.

Example:
Pretend Megan has the *spiritual gift* of being a leader and the *talent* to organize. Then, she can easily put a group together and gather things for someone in need.

3. Can you think of famous people who use their talents to witness for Christ?

You have found the **Treasure**.

 KCKs find and use their gifts and talents to grow a business, build treasure, and help others!

On Your Own

1. Complete *Activity 32: An Income Statement.* File behind *Treasure Builder 1* tab.

2. Learn rule #8 of the **KCK Sales Code**. Say it until you know it.

My KCK Sales Code

8 **I only make promises I can keep.**

3. Update your **KCK Ledger**.

Kingdom Keys

Key to the Lesson

As I use my gifts from God, I will become more confident.

Key Ideas

🔍 **Clue to the Code**
To have a fun career, **KCKs** follow their dreams and develop their gifts.

Character Code
Become Confident

Treasure of the Kingdom
KCKs find and use their gifts and talents to grow a business, build treasure, and help others!

Key Terms

consequence (**kon**-si-kwens) something that happens because of an action

principles (**prin**-suh-pulz) rules and beliefs which guide your thoughts, words, and actions

spiritual gift (**spir**-i-choo-ul) (gift) a special ability given by God

W **Complete *Worksheet 17*:**
Discover Your Gifts.
File behind *Treasure Builder 1* tab.

KCKs, explore your talents while you are young!

CONGRATULATIONS

You may place your Level Seventeen reward on your KCK Treasure Map.

Bonus Code Work

1. What do you want to be doing in ten years? Write the answer in a letter to yourself. Place this letter in an envelope. On the outside of the envelope, write your name and the date it will be ten years from now. Then, put the envelope in a safe place. Open the letter in ten years to see if you have followed your goals and dreams.

2. Read about the spiritual gifts in the Bible. Discuss them with your family or mentor.

Romans 12:3-8
Ephesians 4:11-13
1 Corinthians 12:4-11, 27-28
1 Peter 4:10

3. Think of a time when you had a positive consequence from using your talents. Draw a picture or write a story about that time.

4. Interview your parents, grandparents, older friend, or mentor. Ask them to share important principles learned when they were younger that you need to know. List the principles.

5. Who are your heroes? Draw a picture or write a story about their talents. Share your drawing or story with someone you know.

Lesson 18

What's My Goal?

Proclamation

Jesus tells me everything is possible, if I only believe.

As a child of God, you belong to the greatest family there is! This family is special, because your heavenly Father has a plan for each of His kids. You are one of His kids.

Is there something you want to do or be? Knights, you need to set a goal and work to reach it. Think big! To God, no goal is too big.

Check Your Path

 Begin *Worksheet 18: What's My Goal?*

Quest for the Clue

Is math fun for you?

Do you like to solve problems? Do you enjoy writing transactions in your ledger? If you like working with numbers, then you might want to be a bookkeeper someday. A bookkeeper takes care of the *books* for a company by making entries in the company's ledger.

One of the secrets of a successful business is keeping your books up to date.

Do you remember the weekly goal you set for your business in D-4: Weekly Income Goal of your Business Plan?

It is time to see if you are making more or less money than you planned to make when you set your goal. How can you find out? You will need to **calculate** (**kal**-kyuh-lāt). Calculate means to solve a problem by using math. You will calculate how much money you are making to see if you are meeting your goal.

If your ledger is up to date, then you can calculate your profit or **earnings** (**ur**-ningz), which is money received for work or services. Before you calculate your earnings, you need to know some of the words a bookkeeper uses. Let's get started!

On your mark!

Get set!

Charge!

Sales & Services

To make a sale in your business, you provide a service and collect money for doing the job. When you total all the money you make from your service jobs, it is called your **gross** (grōs) **income**. Gross income is the total amount of money received from sales and services.

Gross Income

Businesses must keep track of their gross income. Many businesses look at it every day, month, or year. Employees look at their gross income when they get paid for their work.

You should calculate your gross income at least once a week to be aware of how much money you are making in your business.

Expenses

Expenses are money spent by your business. There are many different types of expenses, or costs, that a bookkeeper must know. For now, you will *not* need to learn all the different types of expenses to manage your Treasure Builder. Remember, anything that costs money in your business is an expense.

Now you know about sales and services, expenses, and gross income. That's fantastic!

To calculate your profit, there is only one other term you need to know. It is **net income**. Net income is the difference between gross income and expenses.

Net Income

"*What's the bottom line?*" is often asked in business. If you hear this, it means someone wants to know the *net income*.

To find your net income, first add all your income. This is your gross income. Next, add up all your expenses. Then, find the difference between your gross income and expenses to get your net income.

Gross Income
- Expenses
_____
Net Income

Your net income is your profit. If you own a sole proprietorship, it is the total amount of money you have after you pay all your bills. It is your bottom line. It is the money your business keeps after all expenses are paid.

The gross income of a company may be very good, but the business can still be in trouble. How can this happen? If a business *spends* almost as much money as it earns from sales and services, it can make very little money. If it spends *more* money than it earns from sales and services, it may even have a loss.

Where Did My Profit Go?

Knights, pretend you earn $25 from your lawn business one week, but you buy a rake for $24. Your net income for that week is $1. Your gross income of $25 looks good, but after you subtract your expenses, your bottom line looks bad.

Gross Income	$25
- Expenses	-$24
Net Income	$ 1

The next week you earn $40 and have zero expenses. Your net income for the week is $40. The rake was a good purchase, because the rake helped you increase your income. Sometimes businesses *spend* money in order to *make* money.

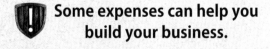
Some expenses can help you build your business.

KCKs, try to make good choices and only spend money on things that your business needs. For example, should you buy colorful work gloves for $30 or a plain pair for $10 if either pair of gloves will work? Always ask, "Is this the right choice for my business?"

You have discovered the **Clue**.

KCKs know how to calculate gross income and net income.

Complete *Activity 33: Net and Weekly Income.*

Code of Honor

What does perseverance mean? Perseverance means you do not give up easily. When you complete a hard job, you feel good about what you have done. Perseverance helps you build a good reputation.

If you keep trying until you finish, you show perseverance.

Have Perseverance

Most people who are successful usually have a lot of perseverance. They keep on trying even when it gets difficult. Knights, follow their examples. Keep your eyes fixed on the goals you are trying to reach. There may be hardships or disappointments along the way, but **keep on keeping on**. It is **The Kingdom Code** way!

Kingdom Code Kids Think Differently!

We set goals and ask God to help us reach them.

What goal would you like to reach? You can do it if you have perseverance. Why? You have an amazing secret weapon (**wep**-uhn). Read the Bible verse to find out what it is.

What then shall we say to these things? If God is for us, who can be against us?
— Romans 8:31 ESV

What secret weapon do you have?

KCKs, you have God on your side!

Let's read a story about a woman who persevered. Her name is **Anne Sullivan**.

❖ History Highlights ❖

Helen Keller could not see or hear. She was in total darkness and total silence. Knights, try to imagine what Helen's world must have been like. Shut your eyes and cover your ears for a moment. How does it feel?

Helen's parents tried to teach her, but they failed. Finally, they hired Anne Sullivan, a woman with great perseverance.

Anne set her goal high. She wanted to remove Helen from a world of darkness. Anne wanted to bring the seven-year-old child into the great world of words and knowledge.

Think how hard it must have been to communicate with Helen. Although it was difficult, Anne taught her sign language and braille (brāyl). Helen could then talk with her hands and read with her fingertips.

Later, Helen was the first deaf-blind student to graduate from college; but Anne had to read most of the textbooks to Helen because the books were not in braille. By using sign language and putting her hand on Anne's face and throat, Helen could "hear" what Anne was reading to her. Anne also taught Helen how to speak.

They traveled all over the world showing others that God-sized dreams can come true.

Helen had disabilities (dis-uh-**bil**-i-tēz), but God gave Anne the gifts and talents to bring Helen into a world of light and understanding. Helen's achievements were a **miracle**, but Anne Sullivan was the **miracle worker**!

Do you think you would like to teach or help someone? There are many professions that deal with teaching or serving others. It may be God's plan for you to be a miracle worker too.

Did you find the **Treasure** that helped Anne Sullivan persevere?

 God blesses people with gifts and talents so they can bless others.

 On Your Own

1. Learn rule #9 of the **KCK Sales Code**.

My KCK Sales Code

I take an adult with me when I make face-to-face sales calls.

Kingdom Keys

Key to the Lesson

With perseverance, I can build treasure, reach my goals, and help others.

Key Ideas

Clue to the Code
KCKs know how to calculate gross income and net income.

Character Code
Have Perseverance

Treasure of the Kingdom
God blesses people with gifts and talents so they can bless others.

Key Terms

calculate (**kal**-kyuh-lāt) to solve a problem by using math

earnings (**ur**-ningz) money received for work or services

gross income (grōs) (**in**-kum) the total amount of money received from sales and services

net income (net) (**in**-kum) the difference between gross income and expenses

I had a Great Week! Hope you did too!

Kingdom Code Kid

Complete *Worksheet 18: What's My Goal?*
File behind *Treasure Builder 1* tab.

CONGRATULATIONS

You may place your Level Eighteen reward on your KCK Treasure Map.

Bonus Code Work

1. Write about a person who had or has a disability. Explain how he or she has overcome the situation.

2. Make a *goal cloud* poster. In the center write a goal you want to reach. Write all the words and thoughts around your goal that will help you succeed. Hang the poster where you will see it everyday.

3. Learn the bookkeeping Key Terms in this lesson. Share what they mean with your family.

4. Think of an area in your life where you need to practice perseverance. For example, if you give up too easily when you start something, keep on practicing until you succeed. Write your needs in your prayer journal, and ask God to help you.

5. Are you happy with your net income? If not, name at least three ways you can increase your bottom line. Draw a chart to show how these ideas can make a difference in your Treasure Builder. Persevere by using these ideas until your net income increases.

Lesson 19

Visiting a Bank

Proclamation

Listen as your teacher reads the *Proclamation*.

I gain knowledge when I have respect for the Lord and His words.

When you read the Bible, search for knowledge like you would search for treasure. After you discover words of wisdom, keep them in your heart. Now, stand and repeat the *Proclamation*.

Check Your Path

 Begin *Worksheet 19: Visiting a Bank.*

Quest for the Clue

Do you remember the first time you received money for a birthday, or earned money for a job you did? What did you do with the money? If you saved your money, did you put it in a piggy bank or a secret place?

Throughout history, people have hidden and saved their money in some crazy places. Now, you can save your money in a bank account, where it is safe and can earn money for you.

In the Middle Ages, all types of coins were made and used for **currency** (**kur**-uhn-sē). Currency is any form of money used for exchange. Many kings, lords, and towns had their own special currency. In fact, there were so many different types of coins that buying and selling became very confusing.

Knowing how to change from one currency to another was not easy to do, but there were professionals who did it well. They were called *money changers*. People paid the money changers a small amount of money to trade their currency for another currency. Then, the people could buy and sell their goods and services more easily.

In Italy, the money changers set up their businesses near markets where people came to buy or sell things. Scales were used to weigh and find the value of coins so one currency could be traded for another.

The money changers sat on benches so people could easily find them.

The word for *bench* in Italian is *banca*. When people went to the money changers sitting on the benches, they went to the banca. Knights, *banca* is where we get the word *bank*!

When you think about a bank, there are two questions you may ask...

Why do I need a bank?

How can I earn money in a bank?

Whoa!

Let's answer one question at a time.

Why Do You Need a Bank?

A bank can be a safe place to keep money. When you put money in a bank, you make a **deposit** (dih-**poz**-it). A deposit is an amount of money put in a bank account. A bank is also a place that loans (lōnz) money. If you borrow money from the bank, you take out a loan.

An **interest** (**in**-ter-ist) **rate** is the amount of money charged or paid for using money. When you put money in some accounts, the bank may *pay* you interest. On the other hand, when you borrow money, you are usually *charged* interest by the bank. Whether you deposit money or borrow money, it is important to compare interest rates because banks have different rates and rules.

❧ Share Your Thoughts ❧

To meet their needs and wants, sometimes people borrow money.

1 Give some good reasons people might need to borrow money.

2 What are some "*not so great*" reasons people want to borrow money?

3 What problems can happen when you borrow from someone?

How Can You Earn Money at a Bank?

Two ways you can earn money at a bank:

• Open a savings account.

• Buy a certificate of deposit.

A savings account keeps your money safe and may pay you an interest rate that can change from day to day. It can often be opened with a small amount of money. Several times a month you are usually allowed to take money out, or **withdraw** (with-**draw**). Withdraw means to remove money from a bank account. The money you take out of an account is called a *withdrawal* (with-**draw**-ul). The number of withdrawals may be different at each bank.

If you save enough money in your savings account, you can invest in a certificate of deposit, which is often called a *CD*. It may take more money to *buy* a CD, but a CD usually pays more interest than a savings account. How does a CD work? You buy a CD for a certain period of time and should not withdraw any of your money during this time. If you make an early withdrawal, you could be fined. CDs usually come with a *set interest rate*. This means the interest rate does not change. At the end of the time period, you get your money back plus the money the CD has earned.

For example, pretend you buy a one-year CD for $1,000. The bank has an interest rate of one percent (1%) per year. At the end of one year, you will earn 1% of $1,000, which is $10. Plus, you get the $1,000 back. That means at the end of one year, you will have $1,010.

1%	of	$1,000	=	$10
Interest Rate		CD Amount		Interest Earned

Two Ways to Save Money

Savings Account	CD
It usually takes a small amount of money to open.	It usually takes a large amount of money to buy.
The interest rate can change daily.	The interest rate usually stays the same.

A savings account and a CD are just two examples of ways you can save money or earn interest at a bank. If you visit a bank, you will be amazed at the many types of accounts there are.

Kingdom Code Kids Think Differently!

Before we open any account, we ask questions to compare rates and rules.

You have found the **Clue**.

A bank is a business where money can be saved, loaned, or exchanged.

Code of Honor

Seek Knowledge

Wisdom and money can protect you. But knowledge gained through wisdom is even better – it can save your life.
— Ecclesiastes 7:12 ERV

KCKs, many people believe money is the only thing that provides safety, but there is a limit to what money can do. God's Word says money can protect you, but knowledge is better. As you grow, try to gain as much knowledge as possible. Your money can be taken away, but your knowledge cannot. How can you gain knowledge through wisdom? You can listen and watch others who are wise. You can also read and discuss the Bible.

Treasure Seeking

In the old days, people sometimes kept their money safe and moved it by using a banking business called *Wells Fargo*.

✛ History Highlights ✛

Wells Fargo was started in 1852 and offered its customers a way to transport money, gold, and valuable items by stagecoach.

The valuables were placed in a treasure box, called a *strong box*, and placed underneath the seat of the stagecoach driver. The drivers were armed and prepared to fight to protect their cargo against robbers. This early way of moving money helped build the trust people put in banks today.

Today, people often put money into a checking account to move it safely from one place to another. It is called a *checking account* because you can write checks to get your money. You can also make deposits or withdrawals from an account with a debit card, credit card, or by using the internet.

If you have your own checking account, it is very important to keep track of the money you **put in** and **take out**. You keep a written record in a book called a *register* (**rej**-uh-ster) or go to the bank's website to see all your transactions. Knights, always know where your money is spent.

At the bank, there are special forms to move money in and out of your account. You can fill out a *deposit slip* to put money in, or use a *withdrawal slip* to take money out.

✛ Action Time ✛

Using play money, set up a make-believe bank where you pretend to open new accounts, make deposits, and make cash withdrawals. You may also set up a make-believe store where people can buy, sell, and write checks. When you buy something at the store, write a check and practice updating your make-believe check register. Store owners can deposit or cash their checks at the make-believe bank.

Always Remember...

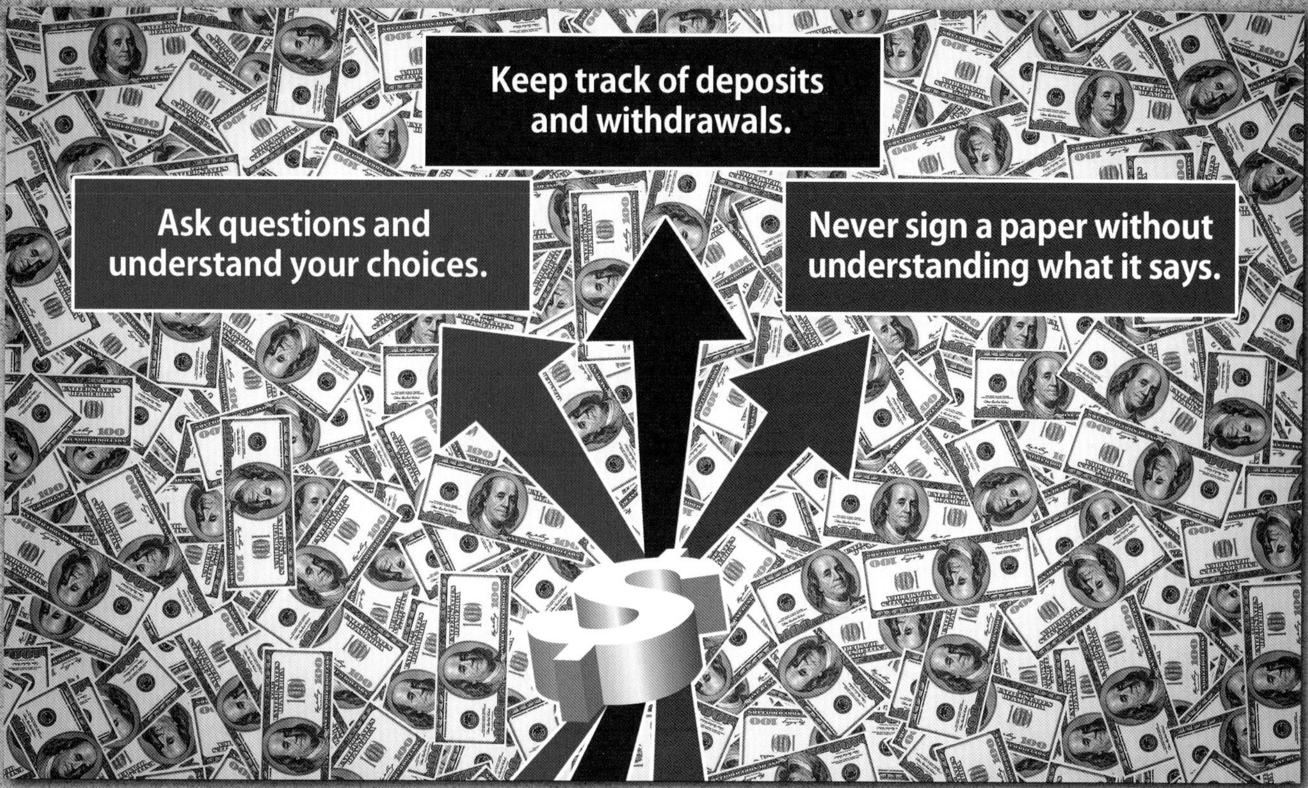

Keep track of deposits and withdrawals.
Ask questions and understand your choices.
Never sign a paper without understanding what it says.

Banking rules can change. Know the rules before making any banking decisions.

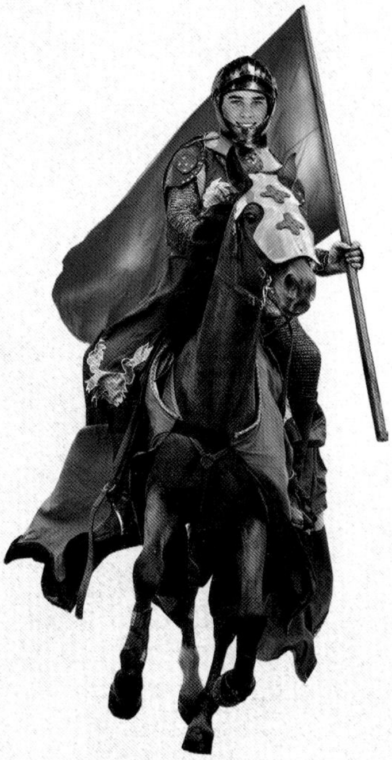

You have found the **Treasure**.

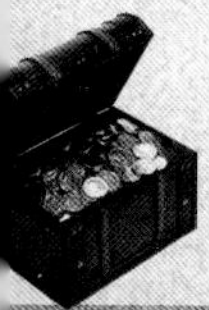

A financial account helps KCKs manage their money easily.

On Your Own

1. Learn rule #10 of the **KCK Sales Code**.

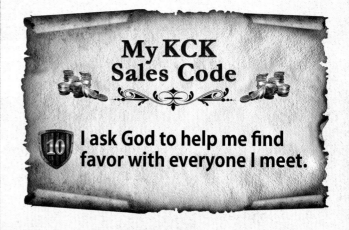

My KCK Sales Code

10 **I ask God to help me find favor with everyone I meet.**

A 2. Complete *Activity 34: Check It Out!* File behind *Treasure Builder 1* tab.

F 3. Use your ledger to complete *Form 4: My Income Statements.* (behind *Forms/Notices* tab) Keep this form with your ledger.

Kingdom Keys

Key to the Lesson

I seek knowledge to be financially responsible.

Key Ideas

Clue to the Code
A bank is a business where money can be saved, loaned, or exchanged.

Character Code
Seek Knowledge

Treasure of the Kingdom
A financial account helps **KCKs** manage their money easily.

Key Terms

currency (**kur**-uhn-sē) any form of money used for exchange

deposit (dih-**poz**-it) 1. (verb) to put money in a bank account 2. (noun) an amount of money put in a bank account

interest rate (**in**-ter-ist) (rāt) the amount of money charged or paid for using money

withdraw (with-**draw**) to remove money from a bank account

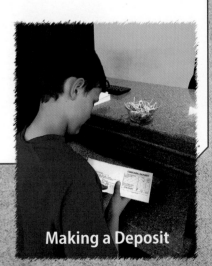

Making a Deposit

Complete *Worksheet 19:*
Visiting a Bank.
File behind *Treasure Builder 1* **tab.**

 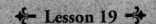

CONGRATULATIONS

You may place your Level Nineteen reward on your KCK Treasure Map.

Bonus Code Work

1. Ask your family to take you with them on their next trip to the bank. While you are there, ask to see deposit and withdrawal slips. Write or tell what you learned.

2. Get a State Identification card. This could be helpful when doing business.

3. Call, email, or visit a bank to complete *Activity 35: Financial Knowledge*. File behind *Treasure Builder 1* tab.

4. Make a flip chart using the ten rules of the **KCK Sales Code**. Use the chart to review the rules. You will need paper, scissors, ruler and a pencil. Have fun with your friends and see who can say the rules first.

Lesson 20

Another Look Back

Proclamation

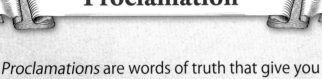

Proclamations are words of truth that give you courage. The more you say them, the more confidence you have. All *Proclamations* in **The Kingdom Code** will help you fight and conquer anything that comes your way!

Knights, look back at Lessons 15 - 19 and find your favorite *Proclamation*. Think about how it can help you overcome problems in your life. Say it every day to give you courage.

Check Your Path

W Begin *Worksheet 20:*
Another Look Back.
You may use your book to find the answers.

Quest for the Clue

When you have a problem, how do you solve it? In the Old Testament, there is a great story about a young man who lived by a code. Let's look at the plan Daniel used when he had to solve a problem that went against his code. His story is quite amazing.

⚜ Historical Fiction ⚜

Daniel's story begins at the time his country was taken over by the king of Babylon. Let's imagine how it might have been for young Daniel and his friends...

"Daniel! Hey, Daniel! Wait up!"

Daniel turned to see his friend coming. He slowed his pace, but kept moving. He knew he had to keep walking.

"Why do you think the king wants us? Do you think he will let us live?" his friend asked Daniel nervously.

"I don't know, but I think he wants us for good, not evil. Our God is my hope, and I trust Him to take care of us."

Daniel was among a group of Jewish young men being taken to Babylon at the order of the king. Once the young men arrived in Babylon, they were taken to the palace. There, they learned the king was training them to serve him. They would be taught the language and ways of their new home and be given food from the king's table. They knew they would be treated very well, but Daniel soon realized he had a big problem!

KCKs, let's look at the first step Daniel took to solve his problem. It is also the first step in the **Problem Solving Plan**.

The problem Daniel spotted was the food. The king required the young men to eat some foods that were not good for them.

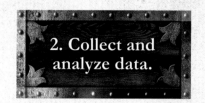

Daniel lived by a code that guided the way he lived and ate. He was taught well by his Jewish parents. As a child, Daniel learned that some food was not healthy to eat. This was the food the young men were being given to eat, by an order from the king. Daniel knew in his heart it was wrong to eat this type of food. After analyzing this data, Daniel felt sure he could plan a strategy.

Daniel believed he and his friends would feel better, think clearer, and be healthier if they ate vegetables and drank water instead of the rich food from the king's table. Daniel had to find a way to carry out his strategy.

4. Find a solution.

Daniel decided there was only one solution. He had to persuade (per-**swād**) the guard to let his friends and him eat plain, natural food.

5. Explain the solution.

Daniel went to the guard and asked him to run a ten-day test. After ten days, Daniel was certain the guard would see a difference between the young men who ate the king's rich food and the Jewish boys who ate only vegetables and water.

6. Decide if it worked.

Ten days passed, and it was time to see if the solution worked. Read the Bible to find out if Daniel was correct.

After the ten days Daniel and his friends looked healthy and well fed. In fact, they looked better than any of the young men who ate the king's food. So the guard didn't require them to eat the king's special food. He didn't require them to drink the king's wine either. He gave them vegetables instead. God gave knowledge and understanding to these four young men. So they understood all kinds of writings and subjects. And Daniel could understand all kinds of visions and dreams.

— Daniel 1:15-17 NIRV

KCKs, let's review the steps of the **Problem Solving Plan** that Daniel used.

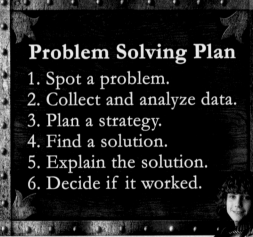

Problem Solving Plan
1. Spot a problem.
2. Collect and analyze data.
3. Plan a strategy.
4. Find a solution.
5. Explain the solution.
6. Decide if it worked.

GOOD JOB!

Now you know the **Clue**.

The Bible gives examples of how to solve problems.

Code of Honor

In the Bible story about Daniel, he was **persuasive** (per-**swā**-siv). Persuasive means being able to convince people to do or believe something. Daniel convinced the guard to let him eat his own food. How? He gave the guard information that was true and could be tested.

Be Persuasive

In the New Testament, Paul was persuasive when he shared the truth about Jesus.

Every Sabbath day he went to the synagogue. He was trying to get both Jews and Greeks to believe in the Lord.
— Acts 18:4 NIRV

Paul wanted to share the truth about Jesus with everyone he met. Even when he was in prison, Paul persuaded others to accept Jesus as their Savior.

When you try to persuade potential customers to buy your service, always use truthful facts and show respect. If people tell you they do not have time to listen, ask them when a more convenient (kuhn-**vēn**-yunt) time would be. They may be in a hurry to get somewhere. Respect their feelings, but do not give up. Set up an appointment for another day.

Knights, timing is very important! This means there is a time to sell, and a time *not* to sell. Ask God for wisdom to know the difference.

Treasure Seeking

You stand in front of the ice cream counter to pick a flavor. Which one will you choose? Do you like strawberry, chocolate, or vanilla? Every day you make choices. Some of those choices are easy; some are not.

For example, your brother or sister wants to play a game that belongs to you. Stop to think about what is important. Make a good choice.

Your friend gets a new bike. You can choose to be excited for your friend or be upset you do not have a new one. It is your choice. Instead of feeling sorry for yourself, a good attitude helps you be happy when your friend gets a new bike.

Someone invites you to see a new movie. You can choose to go to the movie, or complete your school project. You should think about your schedule and what work you must do before you make your decision. If you are choosing between something fun to do and a job to do, it can be a hard choice.

Character Codes help you make good choices. Review the codes from Lessons 15 - 19.

Be Expectant

Being expectant means believing the future is going to be amazing. It is keeping a good attitude when things do not go like you want. Being expectant is knowing God will always take care of you.

Take Initiative

When you take initiative, you finish school projects quickly, do things without being told, and look for ways to please customers. You see things that need to be done, and do them. For example, if someone is washing dishes, you grab a towel and help.

Become Confident

Knights, if you have a good attitude and take initiative, you become confident. Confidence makes it easier to ask others to use your service. Confidence helps you reach your goals.

Have Perseverance

Having perseverance means not giving up and finishing what you start. While you are working hard, you may make a bad decision.

If you make the wrong choice, what can you do? Use your **Problem Solving Plan** to find a solution. Have perseverance instead of giving up. You can overcome any problem if you persevere and have a good attitude.

God will help you find the right path.

Seek Knowledge

Knights, it is always a good choice to seek knowledge. The more you learn, the easier it is to make wise decisions, improve yourself, and help others. Take initiative and seek knowledge to be the best person and proprietor you can be. That is **The Kingdom Code** way!

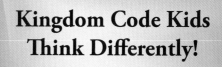

Kingdom Code Kids Think Differently!

We gain confidence by making good choices and persevering.

You have found the **Treasure**.

KCKs live by God's code and make good choices.

On Your Own

1. Say your **KCK Sales Code** out loud. Practice with a friend until you can say all the rules.

Kingdom Keys

Key to the Lesson

I seek knowledge to solve problems and make good choices.

Key Ideas

Clue to the Code
The Bible gives examples of how to solve problems.

Character Code
Be Persuasive

Treasure of the Kingdom
KCKs live by God's code and make good choices.

Key Terms

persuasive (per-**swā**-siv) being able to convince people to do or believe something

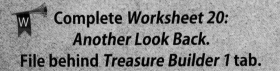

Complete *Worksheet 20:*
Another Look Back.
File behind *Treasure Builder 1* tab.

Your future is shaped by the choices you make and the code by which you live.

CONGRATULATIONS

Place your Level Twenty reward on the KCK Treasure Map!

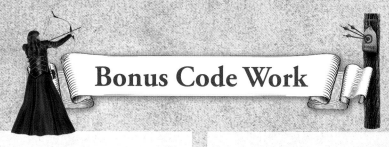

Bonus Code Work

1. Did you write a song to help you remember the **JOEYS** letters of your **KCK Budget**? If you did, add a verse to remind you how much money to put into each *Treasure Keeper*. Practice your jingle and perform it for your class, family, or mentor. If you did not write one, you may write one now and perform it.

2. Do you know someone who is an example of a Character Code? Write an encouraging note to him or her.

3. Knights, think of a problem in your life that needs a solution. Then, use the **Problem Solving Plan** to solve your problem.

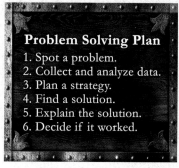

Problem Solving Plan
1. Spot a problem.
2. Collect and analyze data.
3. Plan a strategy.
4. Find a solution.
5. Explain the solution.
6. Decide if it worked.

4. If you have a prayer journal or would like to start one, write about a problem you have. Ask God to help you solve your problem.

Lesson 21

The Pied Piper of Marketing

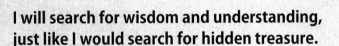

Proclamation

I will search for wisdom and understanding, just like I would search for hidden treasure.

Knights, if you knew there was hidden treasure, how would you search for it? Would you work hard and continue to look, even if it took a long time? Guess what? You should search for wisdom and understanding the same way!

Check Your Path

W Begin *Worksheet 21: The Pied Piper of Marketing.*

Quest for the Clue

Have you heard the story of the Pied Piper? Some say he wore brightly colored clothing; others say he had on hunter's clothes. In every country, the story is told a little differently, but all agree he had a magical pipe or flute...

The Pied Piper showed up from nowhere claiming to be a rat catcher. In a town full of rats, everyone welcomed him.

The city leaders promised the strange man a great amount of money if he would free their city of the horrible rats. So, the Pied Piper walked up and down the streets playing his magical flute. Rats came from every corner to follow the charming sound. The rats followed the Piper out of the town and down into the river, where they all quickly drowned.

The people from the town were thrilled to be rid of the rats, but refused to pay the Piper! This was a huge mistake, and the Pied Piper repaid them in a most cruel way. He walked through the city playing a strange, new tune. Some said it sounded like music from heaven. Others said the music told of a place where bees did not sting, and horses had wings.

No one will ever know the sound the Piper played. The day he played his magical pipe so beautifully was the day he charmed and led the children away... never to be seen again!

KCKs, TV commercials (kuh-**mur**-shulz) and advertisements are like the music of the Pied Piper. Advertisements are written to grab your attention and charm you so you will buy products. Let's look at how this marketing strategy is used to persuade (per-**swād**) people to buy goods and services.

This kind of marketing strategy calls to your **emotions** (e-**mo**-shunz). Emotions are strong feelings inside you. For example, what do you feel when you win a game? How do you feel when your friend is mad at you? Certain events, people, or things you see can cause you to feel good or bad. These feelings are your emotions.

Look at the word cloud below. Have you ever felt any of these emotions?

Sometimes you feel a certain way as you watch a commercial. Your heart may start beating faster, or you may feel hungry. In other words, your emotions and *not your mind*, are responding (ri-**spon**-ding) to what you see. The advertisement or commercial has **emotional** (ē-**mō**-shuh-nl) **appeal** (uh **pēl**). Emotional appeal is advertising with the focus on feelings.

> **Emotional appeal can be very strong. It can make you think you need something because you begin to want it so much.**

Advertisers often use this marketing strategy because they know emotional appeal works. It causes people to buy products.

How does emotional appeal work? If your emotions react (rē-**akt**) to an advertisement, your mind may not question, "*Is this product a good choice for me?*" If you do not judge wisely, you may find yourself quickly buying the product. Knights, that is why you need to always use *common sense* to spot emotional appeal in advertising.

You have found the Clue.

KCKs question advertisements so they can make good choices.

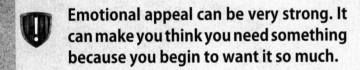

How can you control your emotions and not buy everything that sounds good?

KCKs, seek **discernment** (dih-**surn**-munt). Discernment is the ability to know, understand, and judge correctly. If you can discern what is true and what is false, making good choices becomes easier.

Seek Discernment

And it is my prayer that your love may abound more and more, with knowledge and all discernment.

— Philippians 1:9 ESV

A discerning person keeps wisdom in view...

— Proverbs 17:24a NIV

Discernment helps you know if something is true or if something is good for you.

Sometimes, discernment is just a feeling you have. You cannot explain why you have this feeling, but you **know** the feeling is real. For example, have you ever felt when danger was near? Have you ever been asked to do something you wanted to do, but you felt in your heart it was not right? Guess what? That was discernment! God brings to your *mind* what you know in your *heart* is right.

To know if something is true or if something is good for you, always ask God for discernment. Through the power of the Holy Spirit, spiritual discernment guides you, keeps you safe, and helps you choose wisely.

Kingdom Code Kids Think Differently!

We use discernment before choosing what to buy.

Beware! The Pied Piper of Marketing will call to you in advertisements and commercials like the music called to the children in the story.

Treasure Seeking

Let's discover what makes you buy.

Challenge!

Your quest is to compare and explore the emotions that occur in advertisements.

Six Emotions Used in Advertisements

1. A feeling of power or control, so you believe you can do whatever you want.

2. A feeling that you belong and have lots of friends.

3. A feeling of joy or happiness.

4. A feeling that you are special and deserve to have things.

5. A feeling that you can win or be the best.

6. A feeling of freedom to escape and get away.

Be Detectives!

Look for the emotions above, as you read the following story about the Mighty Mozot...

KCKs, pretend you turn on the TV and there is a new commercial about the Mighty Mozot.

Buy the Mighty Mozot Today!

Kids are dancing, singing, and getting excited about the new product.

Mighty Mozot,
just for me,
I simply have to have one.
Don't you see?
What a wonder
I will be, with my
Mighty Mozot.
I'm sure you agree!

That afternoon, there is another ad. Your favorite sports person tells you how he or she is playing better after buying the Mighty Mozot. You get excited and think, "Maybe if I get one, I'll become a better swimmer. Then, I can be on a team and have lots of friends." You smile and start humming the tune again, "*Mighty Mozot, just for me...*"

For dinner, you go to a restaurant. You cannot believe it. If you buy a certain food, you can get a small, free Mini Mozot. You beg your parents until they buy the meal for you. After playing with the Mini Mozot, you begin to believe you deserve to own the Mighty Mozot. Day after day, you hear about the amazing product. You dream about how it will take you to far away places where great adventures are waiting. A feeling of need is starting to cry out to you.

You open a newspaper, and there is the Mighty Mozot! An idea pops into your mind, "I'll be awesome if I own one of these! I'll be able to do anything I want. I'll be just like all the other kids." You talk to your friends who already own a Mighty Mozot, but they do not seem too excited. It does not matter what they say. You are convinced... you **need** one!

That afternoon, an ad comes on the TV and announces a two-day sale on Mighty Mozots. You have just enough money to buy one at the sale price. You rush to get it. Finally, your dream comes true. You have your very own Mighty Mozot.

For an entire week you play with it every minute of the day. The next week, your Mighty Mozot sits on the shelf. An ad comes on the TV, but you do not listen. You realize you are still the same; nothing has changed. You were charmed by the ads, just like the children who followed the Pied Piper.

Detectives, Now What Do You Feel?

In the Mighty Mozot story, emotional appeal was used as part of the marketing strategy. It was successful because you bought the item. Like metal is drawn to a strong magnet, emotional appeal tugs at consumers' emotions. **KCKs,** advertising is like putting bait in front of fish. Sometimes fish bite; sometimes they do not. Will you, or will you not, take the bait?

Always focus on **why** you want a product. Use discernment. If you practice discernment, you will be a wise consumer.

✦ Share Your Thoughts ✦

Look at the six emotions listed before the story. Make a chart with two columns.

1. In the first column, write the emotions you felt *before* the Mighty Mozot was bought. In the second column, write the emotions you felt *after* it was bought.

2. What questions would have been good to ask the kids who owned a Mighty Mozot?

3. Did a TV commercial ever cause you to buy a product? Share your story.

Knights, you have discovered the Treasure.

KCKs know how to spot emotional appeal in advertisements.

On Your Own

F 1. Update your ledger and complete *Form 4: My Income Statements.* Keep this form with your ledger.

A 2. Complete *Activity 36: Become a Better Buyer.*

Kingdom Keys

Key to the Lesson

I will seek discernment to be aware of emotional appeal in advertising.

Key Ideas

Clue to the Code
KCKs question advertisements so they can make good choices.

Character Code
Seek Discernment

Treasure of the Kingdom
KCKs know how to spot emotional appeal in advertisements.

Key Terms

discernment (dih-**surn**-munt) the ability to know, understand, and judge correctly

emotional appeal (ē-**mō**-shuh-nl) (uh-**pēl**) advertising with the focus on feelings

emotions (ē-**mō**-shunz) strong feelings inside you

W **Complete *Worksheet 21: The Pied Piper of Marketing*** File behind *Treasure Builder 1* tab.

CONGRATULATIONS

You may place your Level Twenty-one reward on the KCK Treasure Map.

Bonus Code Work

1. Make a commercial for an item you would like to have. You can use singing, dancing, or talking that would appeal to a consumer's emotions. Perform your commercial, or have someone record it.

2. List the six emotions used in advertising. Then, take a survey. Ask people which one of the six emotions they think is used the most in advertising. Write which emotion the people chose the most. Tell why you think it was chosen most often.

3. Paint or draw pictures that remind you of an emotion. It can be love, anger, joy, or any other emotion you choose.

4. Using a newspaper or magazine, find an ad for each one of the six emotions that cause people to buy. Cut out the advertisements, and place all of them on a poster. Label each advertisement with the emotion used.

Lesson 22

How Do Economies Grow?

Proclamation

Whatever gifts God has given me, I will use to help others.

Think about the spiritual gifts and talents you have been given. **KCKs**, your gifts from God are your resources. How can you use them to help others?

Check Your Path

Begin *Worksheet 22: How Do Economies Grow?*

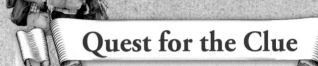

Quest for the Clue

When you study the history of any successful economy, you can learn how to make the economy where you live grow stronger. Let's take a look at the economy of the state where Aunt Jimmi lives.

Did you know people from all over the world built the Texas economy? The state grew from Native Americans hunting and gathering the available resources around them to the busy economy Texans enjoy today.

⊹ History Highlights ⊹

Texas has many legends (**lej**-unds) in its history. Stories of cowboys, oil companies, and huge ranches are often made into movies. Are any of these stories true? Take a look at the history of Texas, and then you decide.

Texas, From the Beginning...

The first people who came to Texas found an amazing resource. This resource provided almost all of the things they needed: food, clothing, housing, tools, dishes, fuel for fires, and materials to make jewelry. These things came from one resource:

- It was the largest land animal in North America.

- It ate grass on the plains of Texas.

- It roamed North America in large herds.

Can you guess the name of this amazing resource?

If you guessed bison or buffalo, you are correct!

The early natives of Texas hunted the plentiful buffalo for many years. They used every part of the animal, even its funny-looking tail.

Besides buffalo, the land was full of other natural resources people could hunt and  gather. Nuts, fruits, berries, and roots were gathered from the land. Fish, clams, and mussels came from rivers and ocean.

The Native Americans later grew corn, squash, melons, and beans in parts of Texas where the soil was ideal for raising crops.

People came from regions all over the world to settle territory that later became the state of Texas. Texas, known as the *Lone Star State*, attracted many **immigrants** (**im**-i-grents). Immigrants are people who leave one country to make a new home in another country. Immigrants came to North America and Texas for different reasons, but they all came to meet their needs and wants. To discover why immigrants came, let's look at the six countries who ruled over Texas.

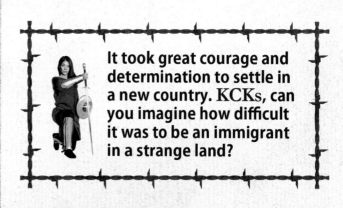

It took great courage and determination to settle in a new country. KCKs, can you imagine how difficult it was to be an immigrant in a strange land?

Challenge!

Discover how the history and economy of Texas was shaped by each country whose flag flew over Texas.

The Six Flags That Flew Over Texas

The **Spanish flag** was the first flag to fly over the land that later became Texas.

In the 1500s, Spain was a strong country with many ships. Explorers were sent to the New World to find both land and riches to expand the empire of Spain. Besides searching for new resources, the Spanish also sent priests to spread **Christianity** (kris-chē-**an**-i-tē). Christianity is the religion which teaches and believes Jesus is the Son of God and the Savior of the world.

Priests from Spain founded about thirty-five missions in Texas. Longhorn cattle were brought by the priests to provide food as they traveled and established (ih-**stab**-lisht) the missions.

In the missions, priests lived with the Native Americans and shared Christ with them. The priests also taught them how things were done in Europe.

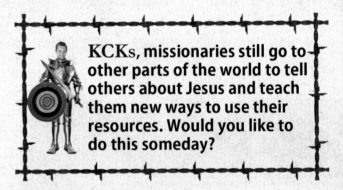

KCKs, missionaries still go to other parts of the world to tell others about Jesus and teach them new ways to use their resources. Would you like to do this someday?

The **French flag** was the second flag to fly over the territory that later became Texas.

Even though Spain claimed Texas, there were very few people from Spain living in Texas except the priests. So, when the French came to explore the vast land, it was easy for them to settle part of the region without bothering the Spanish.

The French set up trade routes and trading posts. These trading posts opened up new territory to be settled. Why? People could now buy goods from the trading posts and move into undeveloped (un-di-**vel**-upt) land. As more and more people came, the Texas economy grew.

The third flag to fly over the land of Texas was the **Mexican flag**.

After Mexico won its independence from Spain, the Mexican flag replaced the Spanish flag over Texas. Pioneers from Mexico moved north to Texas to protect the land Mexico now owned. Mexican settlers brought new types of food, clothing, and farming ideas that changed the economy of Texas.

The Mexican government decided to offer cheap land to Anglo-Americans, who were people from America that spoke English.

One Anglo-American, Stephen F. Austin, led 300 families from the young United States and settled along the Brazos River. These families became known as the *Old Three Hundred*. They wanted a new life and cheap land. They bought land for about four cents an acre!

After the *Old Three Hundred* settled the land, the Mexican government allowed more people to come farm, ranch, and develop **commerce** (**kom**-ers). Commerce is business or trade. Laws were made to let Anglo-Americans settle the state, but Mexicans had first choice of the land. The Anglo-Americans were offered cheap land and no taxes. The deal was great, and settlers poured in!

These settlers were true entrepreneurs who set up their own economy. Without many rules to hinder them, they worked hard to farm and ranch the land. Their success made people from other countries want the same opportunity for themselves.

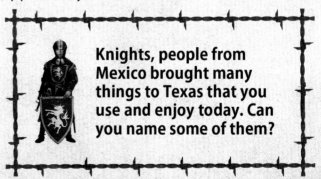

Knights, people from Mexico brought many things to Texas that you use and enjoy today. Can you name some of them?

The **Republic of Texas flag** was the fourth flag to fly over Texas.

The great business deal Mexico offered to settlers did not last forever. The Mexican leader, Santa Anna, along with some rich landowners, changed the laws. They took away the settlers' freedoms.

The settlers were mad, fighting mad! They decided to defend their rights and go to war with Santa Anna. The most famous battle fought in this war took place at a mission in San Antonio at the *Battle of the Alamo*. At the Alamo, men fought and died to gain their freedom from Mexico.

In 1836, Texas won its freedom and became its own country, the Republic of Texas.

The **Confederate flag** was the fifth flag to fly over Texas.

The Republic of Texas joined the United States of America and became the state of Texas in 1845. Sixteen years later, Texas joined the Confederacy (kun-**fed**-er-uh-sē) and fought against the United States for many reasons. For example, the Texas economy depended on farming cotton and working slaves. This war, known as the Civil War, ended in 1865.

During the war, the Texas economy fell apart. Why? The war cost a lot of money and used many resources. The war also took men away from their homes and businesses.

After the Civil War, the **United States flag** again flew over the state to become the sixth flag, but the Texas economy needed help.

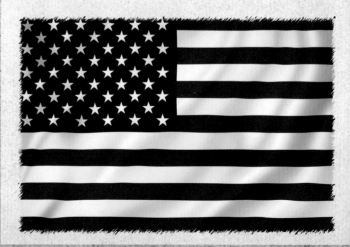

There was one resource in large supply after the war, and it helped rebuild the economy. Can you guess what it was?

Wild Longhorn Cattle

Cattle were often left to roam the land while ranchers were at war, so many herds grew very large during the Civil War. Then, after the war, entrepreneurs and cattlemen rounded up the wild longhorns for their ranches. They also began selling beef to other parts of the country. Over time, the cattle industry grew to be a major part of the state's economy.

Texas had other resources besides cattle. A few of them were rich soil for farming, seafood from the Gulf of Mexico, forests, oil, and natural gas. Over the years, hard working people used these and other resources to rebuild a strong economy in the state.

You now know the **Clue**.

🔍 **A great economy can grow when available resources are used.**

Code of Honor

Be Resourceful

If you are hungry, what do you do?

- Look in the refrigerator.
- Pick something from the garden.
- Go to a restaurant.

When you find something to eat, you are being **resourceful** (rē-**sōrs**-ful). Resourceful means finding clever ways to meet needs and wants.

Kingdom Code Kids Think Differently!

We are aware of the resources God provides, and we use them wisely.

Share Your Thoughts

One way to be resourceful is to be aware of the things God has given you. Did you know you were put on this earth to take care of God's land? Let's see what the Bible says.

The Lord God took the man and put him in the Garden of Eden to work it and take care of it.

— Genesis 2:15 NIV

1. What free resources are available to you?

2. How can you use these resources?

3. How can you take care of the resources around you?

?

Treasure Seeking

The many resources and opportunities in North America drew immigrants from every corner of the world. They came to the New World in search of freedom and the chance to succeed in business. Immigrants also brought different **occupations** (ock-yuh-**pā**-shuns). An occupation is the work a person does to earn a living.

About 6,000 immigrants from Germany came to Texas and settled in New Braunfels and Fredericksburg. At that time in Germany, the people did not have the freedom to practice capitalism or the freedom to worship as they pleased. In Texas, they could do both.

Czech (chek) immigrants came to farm the rich soil of the upper coastal plain in Texas. Also, Asian immigrants came to the Texas coast where they could fish for shrimp as they had in their old country.

Chinese immigrants came to Texas to build railroads. The railroads opened up commerce so products from different areas could be sold or traded more easily. Many Chinese settled in the city of Houston and opened goods and service businesses. Japanese immigrants also settled near Houston and grew rice on land perfectly suited for growing this crop.

Immigrants brought all types of occupations from many countries. They also developed the resources in Texas through hard work. As the Texas economy grew, so did commerce between Texas and the rest of the world.

You have found the **Treasure**.

A great economy is made when people with many skills and talents have the freedom to live and work together.

On Your Own

1. Immigrants brought many changes to the economy and culture. What have immigrants brought to your community?

Write a paragraph, give a presentation, or make a poster about something that came from another country. For example: food, clothes, sports, toys, art, or music. Give the country it came from, and tell whether it fills a *want* or a *need*.

2. Prepare for Lesson 23. Copy the chart below. Under **Needs**, list all the things you need to survive. Under **Wants**, list everything else. File the chart behind *Treasure Builder 1* tab.

What's in My Bedroom?	
Needs	**Wants**
blanket	bed

Kingdom Keys

Key to the Lesson

I have the freedom to be part of a great economy, and will be resourceful with my talents and skills.

Key Ideas

Clue to the Code
A great economy can grow when available resources are used.

Character Code
Be Resourceful

Treasure of the Kingdom
A great economy is made when people with many skills and talents have the freedom to live and work together.

Key Terms

Christianity (kris-chē -**an**-i-tē) the religion which teaches and believes Jesus is the Son of God and the Savior of the world

commerce (**kom**-ers) business or trade

immigrants (**im**-i-grents) people who leave one country to make a new home in another country

occupation (ock-yuh-**pā**-shun) the work a person does to earn a living

resourceful (rē-**sōrs**-ful) finding clever ways to meet needs and wants

 Complete *Worksheet 22: How Do Economies Grow?*
File behind *Treasure Builder 1* **tab.**

CONGRATULATIONS

You may place your **Level Twenty-two** reward on the KCK Treasure Map.

Bonus Code Work

1. How are the resources near you used?

2. Research to find how Native Americans used all the different parts of the bison. Then, create a poster or a visual presentation.

3. Read about an old mission. It could be in Texas or anywhere in the United States. Build a model of the mission with blocks, clay, or other materials. Share your model and what you learned with someone.

4. Write historical fiction. Have your story, play, or movie be about an immigrant who settled your state. Be sure your story includes both facts from history and your own ideas of what might have happened.

Lesson 23

Take Charge of Your Life!

Proclamation

I will focus on the things of God, and trust Him to take care of me.

Right now, do you really *need* anything? If you do, can you trust your Heavenly Father to supply it? Yes, you can, because Jesus gave you a promise. You must **ask** in the name of Jesus and **believe**.

> *Whatever you ask in my name, this I will do, that the Father may be glorified in the Son.*
>
> — John 14:13 ESV

Check Your Path

Begin *Worksheet 23: Take Charge of Your Life!*

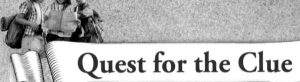

Quest for the Clue

What is the difference between something you need and something you want? **Needs** are things a person must have to survive. **Wants** are things a person desires but does not need to survive.

❧ Share Your Thoughts ❧

Remember the chart: *What's in My Bedroom?* Discuss things found in a bedroom that could be *needs* and *wants*.

1. What could be a *need*?

2. What could be a *want*?

3. Are there more *wants* than *needs*?

?

From: *Aunt Jimmi*

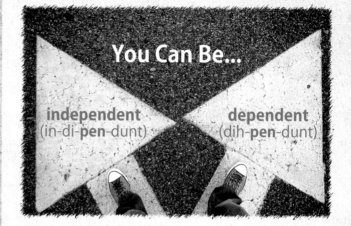

You Can Be...

independent
(in-di-**pen**-dunt)

dependent
(dih-**pen**-dunt)

Dear Kingdom Code Kids,

When I was very young, my father told me about Needmore. He would say to me, "When Needmore is knocking at the door, you have to work and do whatever it takes so he'll go away."

I really thought there was a man named Needmore. I pictured him as a bony old man in a long black coat reaching his skinny finger out of his sleeve and pecking on our door. I was terrified I might meet him one day! In fact, I would have done anything to keep him away. Needmore was very real to me.

It was many years later when I finally understood what my Dad was trying to tell me.... If you <u>need more</u> money, you must work, maybe even work more than usual to earn it.

During my lifetime, I have seen people work at two or more jobs to keep food on the table for their families and pay their bills. I admire these brave people. They don't sit around and complain. No way! They work hard.

Knights, if Needmore ever comes knocking at your door, drive him away with hard work. You can do it.

I believe in you!
Aunt Jimmi

Independent means to be free, rely on oneself, and to think or act for oneself.

Dependent means to be under the control of another, or to rely on someone or something else.

How Can You Be Independent?

If Needmore comes knocking at your door, take initiative and provide for yourself.

- Know what needs to be done and do it.
- Choose to work and earn money.
- Do more than what is expected.

 Be independent by showing initiative and choosing to work.

How Can You Become Dependent?

If Needmore is at the door, sometimes people borrow money, use a credit card, ask others for help, or seek government aid. This is only a way to live for a short time. If Needmore knocks you down, you need to get back on your feet. Being dependent should never become a way of life if you are able to work.

What can happen if you continue to depend on others for your needs and wants? You may never use your God-given talents. You can miss the joy of a fun career. You might not be the world changer God wants you to be. Always try to work and meet your own needs.

Kingdom Code Kids Think Differently!

We choose to work when Needmore is knocking at the door.

God is your source, and He will take care of you. If you need a good strategy to succeed financially, pray and ask God for ways to earn money. Then, take action. That is **The Kingdom Code** way!

How can you take action? **KCKs**, after you find a way to earn money, be expectant. Step out in faith. Work to make it happen.

Many people learn ways to overcome their disabilities (dis-uh-**bil**-i-tēz) in order to be able to work. What warriors!

Knights, you must learn to overcome any problems you face now or in the future. How do you overcome and become a winner?

- ⭐ **Pray for guidance.**
- ⭐ **Show initiative.**
- ⭐ **Work hard.**
- ⭐ **Persevere.**

Now you know the **Clue**.

🔍 **Hard work leads to independence!**

But my God shall supply all your need according to his riches in glory by Christ Jesus.

— Philippians 4:19 KJV

Have Faith

✦ Share Your Thoughts ✦

1. Share a time when God met your needs.

2. Why is it better to be *independent* instead of *dependent*?

3. What can you do now, so you can be independent in the future?

4. How can you help others if Needmore is at their door?

By helping others...
...we help ourselves.

In your day-to-day living, God blesses you with the ability to make choices about your **wants** and **needs**.

For example when you shop and find things you want, you check to see if you have enough money to buy them. Then ask yourself...

Do I really need this?

Why do I want this?

God gives you the ability to question what you really **need**. If you question, you can keep from impulse buying when you shop.

Choices

In the free enterprise system, a consumer has the benefits of many choices and opportunities to spend money. **KCKs**, this is what makes saving your money so difficult!

For example, have you ever noticed how many different choices of dog food there are?

You can buy dog food for small breeds, large breeds, old dogs, and puppies. Many choices are available. If you do not like any of them, you have the opportunity to visit other stores or feed your dog table scraps. The choices are yours to make.

Knights, businesses attract consumers with emotional appeal. Remember all the ways they try to lure you to buy their products? You have to wisely decide if you *want* or *need* their items.

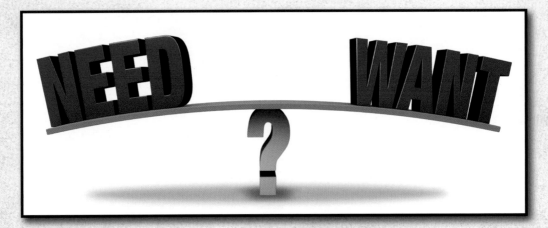

Through advertising, businesses try to make you think you **need** what they sell.
Their marketing strategy is to create a desire in your *mind*, so you will want to buy their products.
The emotional appeal may be great, but KCKs, you are stronger. Shop wisely!

In your mind, you can sometimes turn wants into needs.

Question: Why would someone do that?

Answer: To make it OK to buy something that is *wanted*, but not really *needed*.

There are always things you will want to buy to improve your Treasure Builder. Be aware of the difference between a need or a want in your business. Extra purchases take away the profit from your business.

Have you ever wanted something so much that you convinced yourself you needed it?

Knowing the difference between what you *need* and what you *want* helps you:

• **Choose wisely when you shop.**
• **Manage money God's way.**
• **Keep a profit in your Treasure Builder.**

You have discovered the **Treasure**.

 KCKs choose wisely because they know the difference between needs and wants.

On Your Own

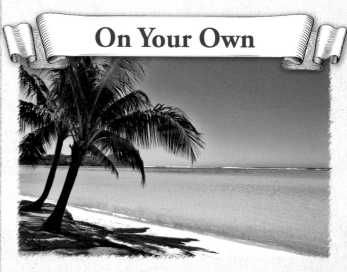

Food, shelter, clothing, and water are needed for you to survive. Things often become clearer when you are placed in an extreme situation (like being stranded on a deserted island). You realize what your needs really are.

 1. Complete *Activity 37: Stranded on a Deserted Island.*

 2. Update your ledger and complete *Form 4: My Income Statements.* Keep this form with your ledger.

Kingdom Keys

Key to the Lesson

I have faith in God to help me make good choices about my future, so I can be independent.

Key Ideas

🔍 **Clue to the Code**
Hard work leads to independence!

Character Code
Have Faith

Treasure of the Kingdom
KCKs choose wisely because they know the difference between needs and wants.

Key Terms

dependent (dih-**pen**-dunt) to be under the control of another; to rely on someone or something else

independent (in-di-**pen**-dunt) to be free; rely on oneself; to think or act for oneself

Take pride in your work by doing a good job.

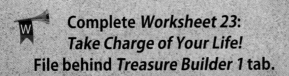

Complete *Worksheet 23: Take Charge of Your Life!* File behind *Treasure Builder 1* tab.

CONGRATULATIONS

You may place your Level Twenty-three reward on the KCK Treasure Map.

Bonus Code Work

1. Make up a song giving the four ways to overcome problems and be a winner:

- Pray for guidance.
- Show initiative.
- Work hard.
- Persevere.

2. Draw or tell about a person who had to persevere to get a job.

3. When you took inventory of your bedroom, did you find things you no longer need or want? If you did, this is a great time to give some away! God blesses those who share with others in need.

Donation box   Donation box

4. Interview someone who has a disability but chooses to work. Ask what hardships he or she faces while trying to be independent.

Lesson 24

Are You Free to Make Choices?

Proclamation

I will be honest in words and deeds so I can be a shining light to others.

Pretend you are on a dark path and turn on a flashlight. Imagine how good it feels to see what is ahead. Like the light shining on a path, honest words and actions can make others feel good about you. Speak the truth and be honest, so your light will shine for others.

Check Your Path

W Begin *Worksheet 24: Are You Free to Make Choices?*

Quest for the Clue

Have you ever seen a tiger pace back and forth in a cage? Why do you think he does it? Do you think he wants to be free so he can choose where he goes and what he eats? **KCKs**, when you get up in the morning, can you choose to get dressed, brush your teeth, or go to the kitchen? If the answer is *yes*, then you have the gift of freedom to make choices. You are not like the tiger in the cage; you are independent.

People can usually choose to be dependent or independent. However, there are times when people believe help and money should be given to them for free. This is called **entitlement** (en-**tī**-tl-munt). Entitlement is a feeling or belief that you deserve to be given something. Entitlement can make a person depend on others, but sometimes people really **do** need help from others.

Entitlement programs can help people who honestly qualify (**kwol**-uh-fī) and deserve it.

Government aid programs were created to help people meet their needs. Perhaps people cannot work because they are mentally or physically not able to work. When people truly qualify, they should receive money or aid.

The problem is this: not everyone is honest.

People sometimes do not tell the truth to receive free goods, services, and money from entitlement programs. Some people choose to receive aid instead of earning a living. They think it is the easy way. What they do not realize is that if they make this choice, it limits their opportunities to improve the way they live in the future. They can quickly become dependent on others to take care of them and lose their work skills.

When people get money from government aid programs by giving false information, they steal from honest people. How?

People pay the government money called **taxes** (**taks**-iz). Taxes are required payments of money to state or federal governments.

- Businesses pay taxes on all the profits they make.

- Employees pay taxes on money they earn.

- Consumers pay taxes on some goods and services they buy.

KCKs, when tax is added to something you buy, it is called *sales tax* and is paid to the government. So, if people lie to get money from the government, they are actually stealing from you and others who obey the law and pay their taxes.

The Story of the Tiger in the Cage

Pretend you are like a tiger in a cage, and depend on others to feed and take care of you. At first it seems nice, and you are very content. There are few worries. You get comfortable and cozy. You get used to having free things. Then one day, you want more food and the opportunity to go get it, but you are trapped. You start pacing and growling, because you realize an important truth.

When people choose not to work and depend on others to provide their finances, they choose to live like a tiger in a cage. It is very easy for them to lose their independence.

When you depend on someone else to provide your needs and wants, you give up your freedom!

You want to be free to:

• **Earn as much money as you can.**

• **Make your own decisions.**

• **Choose a career you enjoy.**

• **Improve the way you live.**

• **Be independent.**

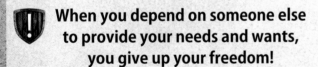

Knights, because you live in a free enterprise system, you have the opportunity to work and earn money. You are entitled to choose the career you want and improve your life. Capitalism gives you the right to be an entrepreneur and start your own business.

From: *Aunt Jimmi*

Dear Kingdom Code Kids,

I once had a friend who had one goal: to get off government entitlement programs. She had six children and lived in government housing. Her dream was to own a home and not have to depend on the government.

She bought second-hand clothes for her children, got movies from the library, and saved money every way she could. To me, she was a world changer!

Did she ever get off the government aid programs? Yes she did, but it was not easy. She worked for years to reach her goal. She persevered. With God's help, she got out of the cage and became free.

Many people feel trapped, but with time and perseverance, they can become independent. I know. I saw it happen!

Have faith,
Aunt Jimmi

Code of Honor

Integrity is being honest, truthful, and doing what is right. If you have integrity, you never cheat or steal from others. When you make a promise, you keep it. You always treat others with respect, and you always play fair. You are a good sport, even when it is very difficult. This is **The Kingdom Code** way!

Have Integrity

❧ Action Time ❧

Create a make-believe play or story about an animal in a cage that gets tired of depending on others. Show or tell how it gets its freedom.

Then, show the animal teaching other animals about ways to prepare for their future. For example, the animal could tell about using talents, saving money, or getting an education.

You have found the **Clue**.

🔍 **KCKs choose to be independent and tell the truth.**

You must not steal. You must not cheat people. You must not lie to each other.
— Leviticus 19:11 ERV

After you finish a service job, how do you feel when your customer is happy and you earn money? This feeling is **pride** (prīd). Pride is a feeling of happiness that comes from doing something well.

It is awesome to take pride in your work!

KCKs, as you earn money in your Treasure Builder, you can take pride because you are becoming financially responsible.

You are financially responsible and feel pride when you:

- Give customers correct change.
- Save money earned from your service business.
- Keep your ledger up to date.
- Make wise choices when you buy something needed in your business.

You also feel pride when you practice integrity at home, at school, and wherever you go. You cannot turn integrity on and off like a faucet. Having integrity should be a way of life.

Kingdom Code Kids Think Differently!

We take pride in working hard and being financially responsible.

Pride comes from a job well done. Whether you are earning money or just helping a friend, always do your best.

Share Your Thoughts

Let's look at times when it might be difficult to take pride in your work and show integrity.

1. The clock says you should leave for your next service job, but you are on the last level to win a game. What do you do?

2. You are playing with your little sister for an hour to help your mom. Your friend invites you to come over. What do you do?

3. It is your responsibility to take out the trash, but you overslept and are late for school. What do you do?

4. Share a time when it was difficult for you to choose the right thing to do.

You have found the **Treasure**.

KCKs show integrity and take pride in their work.

On Your Own

1. Enter all of your transactions into your **KCK Ledger**.

2. Write or draw a picture about a time when you worked, and felt pride after you finished the job.

Kingdom Keys

Key to the Lesson

I will have integrity and work with pride to meet my needs and keep my freedom.

Key Ideas

Clue to the Code
KCKs choose to be independent and tell the truth.

Character Code
Have Integrity

Treasure of the Kingdom
KCKs show integrity and take pride in their work.

Key Terms

entitlement (en-**tī**-tl-munt) a feeling or belief that you deserve to be given something

pride (prīd) a feeling of happiness that comes from doing something well

taxes (**taks**-iz) required payments of money to state or federal governments

Ask God to use you as a shining light.

W Complete *Worksheet 24:*
Are You Free to Make Choices?
File behind *Treasure Builder 1* tab.

CONGRATULATIONS

You may place your Level Twenty-four reward on the KCK Treasure Map.

Bonus Code Work

1. Write a note of encouragement to someone who has done something to help you or has made a difference in your life.

Dear Mrs. Cole,

Thank you for encouraging me when math seemed way too hard.

MaKenzie

2. Almost every time you buy something, you pay sales tax. Find how much the sales tax rate is in your community.

3. Write down four items you want. Choose at least two that cost over $100. Research to find the best price and the sales tax for each item.

4. Interview or research someone who operates a successful business. Write the answers to the following questions:

- What made him or her successful?
- Does the business sell goods or services?
- What was the hardest thing about starting the business?
- How does the business advertise?

5. With your parent's or teacher's permission, go online to www.irs.gov to read about the history of the Internal Revenue Service. Share what you learn with someone.

Lesson 25

Watch Your Pennies!

Proclamation

I will put my Heavenly Father's Kingdom first and do what He wants me to do.

Knights, put the Heavenly Father's Kingdom first. How? Believe that Jesus died for your sins so you can live forever in heaven. Let God be first in your life. Tell others about Christ and His love. Read and follow the words of the Bible. Then, treat others like you want to be treated.

Now, stand and repeat the *Proclamation*.

Check Your Path

Begin *Worksheet 25: Watch Your Pennies!*

Quest for the Clue

Do you ever have *the wants* when you see something? *The wants* are emotions and thoughts that tempt you to impulse buy. The choice you make when you have *the wants* affects the money you have.

If you buy everything you want, you will quickly run out of money.

Let's read a letter from Aunt Jimmi, who learned early in life how to handle *the wants*. She learned to be **thrifty** (**thrif**-tē). Thrifty means carefully using money and other resources. Look for the *two words* in her letter that can help you become thrifty.

From: Aunt Jimmi

Dear Kingdom Code Kids,

My parents taught me a secret. When we had very little money, we practiced the secret. After we had more, we still practiced it. It is only two words, but if you do it, you will be a financial winner. Ready for the secret? _Make do_!

Let me tell you some of the ways my family learned to _make do_. We cooked, ate at home, and used leftovers instead of going out to eat. As a bonus, I learned how to cook. My mother knew how to sew and made my clothes, but I got to design them. We played lots of board games, card games, and dominoes instead of going to expensive places for our entertainment. These games taught me how to form strategies, which later helped me in my businesses. I did not have high-priced shoes or name-brand jeans. I did not even ask for them because I knew we could not afford them. We used coupons and waited for sales to buy the things we needed. Looking for bargains was a game to me. I had a feeling of pride whenever I found a good deal.

You want to know something crazy? We were happy. We were really, really happy! Why? Instead of looking at what we did _not_ have; we looked at what we _did_ have.

I always knew God was with us and would take care of us. He did! With hard work and being thrifty, we made it through some rough times. Knights, you may be having some tough times at home

right now. If you are, help your parents _make do_. On the other hand, if your life is without a worry, it is still a good time to practice making do! Either way, if you are thrifty, you are a financial winner.

Bless you,
Aunt Jimmi

Make Do!

These words are simple to remember, but not always easy to follow. How can you _make do_?

- **Only buy things you can afford.**
- **Use the resources you own or can find.**
- **Repair and take care of things so they last.**
- **Be happy with what you have.**

If you have peace in your heart and mind, the little voice in your head saying, "I want this or that," will not control you. Always let little things bring you joy.

 Have fun, and keep a good attitude as you _make do_.

✦ Action Time ✦

 Present a skit. Pretend you are doing one of the things Aunt Jimmi's family did to be thrifty, or use an idea of your own. In the skit, show someone with a good attitude and someone with a bad attitude. Have fun.

Did you find the **Clue**?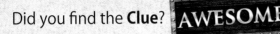

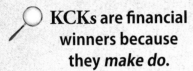

🔍 **KCKs are financial winners because they *make do*.**

🎺 Complete *Activity 38: How to "Make Do"*.

Code of Honor

Become Thrifty

Let's read to find what the Bible says about being thrifty.

..., you should watch what the ants do and learn from them. Ants have no ruler, no boss, and no leader. But in the summer, ants gather all of their food and save it. So when winter comes, there is plenty to eat.
— Proverbs 6:6b-8 ERV

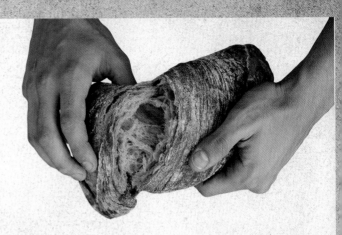

There is another story in the Bible about being thrifty. Do you remember when Jesus fed 5,000 people with five loaves of bread and two fish? Your quest is to read and discover how Jesus gave an example of being thrifty.

Then Jesus took the loaves and gave thanks. He handed out the bread to those who were seated. He gave them as much as they wanted. And he did the same with the fish.

When all of them had enough to eat, Jesus spoke to his disciples. "Gather the leftover pieces," he said. "Don't waste anything." So they gathered what was left over from the five barley loaves. They filled 12 baskets with the pieces left by those who had eaten.
— John 6:11-13 NIRV

✦ Share Your Thoughts ✦

1. After Jesus performed a great miracle with available resources, what did Jesus say to His disciples?

2. What do you think the disciples did with the twelve baskets of leftovers?

3. Discuss how you can be thrifty at home. How can you save money in these areas?

   • entertainment (en-ter-**tān**-munt)
   Examples of being thrifty: Play games, and watch movies at home.

   • clothes

   • food and drinks

   • school supplies

   • gifts you give

   • **utilities** (ū-**til**-i-tēs) Utilities are services that are provided to the public.
   Examples of being thrifty with utilities: Turn off lights, and do not waste water.

4. Share about a time when you had *the wants*. Tell where you were and what you were doing. What can you do the next time you feel *the wants*?

?

Treasure Seeking

Do you like to shop? Let's pretend you are at home when Grandma says to you, "Saving pennies here and there can turn into dollars in your pocket! Remember this when you go shopping today."

Later, you and your mom go to the grocery store. She opens her purse, and pulls out her coupons.

Mom grabs a cart and starts down the first aisle. She chooses two cans of vegetables that have the store-brand label. You ask why she got them instead of the cans with a nice picture on them. She replies, "I've tried both, and they both taste good. Why should we pay more for the pretty labels?" She writes down something on a note pad.

You notice your mother puts some cans in the cart with name-brand labels, but does not write on her note pad.

Next, you go down the row with all the cereals. On the shelf, just at your eye-level, you spot your favorite one. You grab the box! Your mom tells you to put it back. She reaches up to the top shelf and pulls down a big bag of cereal. It is not in a box with bright colors on it. She writes again on the note pad.

Then, she heads straight for the fruits and vegetables. You really love apples. She picks up several and turns them over and over to look at them, but she keeps putting the apples back. She buys bananas and says, "This week the apples have brown spots. Besides, bananas are on sale." She writes again.

This has been a disappointing trip for you. *Your mom has not bought one thing you wanted.*

As you walk to the car, she takes out her note pad and hands it to you. It has a total of $1.82 on it. She says, "That's how much I saved today by making smart buying choices." She takes one dollar and eighty-two cents from her purse and hands it to you. "Now," she says, "put this in your *Y Treasure Keeper*. It will get you a little closer to buying that game you want."

You feel the money in your pocket, and remember what Grandma said about the pennies. They really do add up to make dollars! A smile appears on your face, and you decide the cereal and bananas will taste just fine.

When you are aware of where your money goes, you can make it go further!

KCKs, prepare for the future. Be thrifty! Why? You will have more money for...

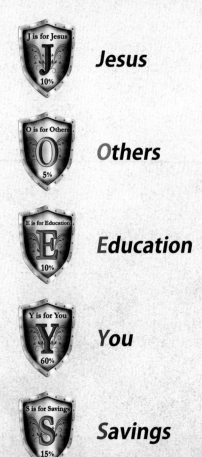

J is for Jesus
10%
Jesus

O is for Others
5%
Others

E is for Education
10%
Education

Y is for You
60%
You

S is for Savings
15%
Savings

Tip: When you are shopping, if you choose to spend your money on everything you see, you will never have enough money to buy what you really need or want.

Kingdom Code Kids Think Differently!

We make good choices and spend our money wisely.

You just found the **Treasure**.

KCKs make good choices when they spend their money.

On Your Own

1. Update your ledger. Be sure all the money you have earned and every expense is written down. Complete *Form 4: My Income Statements.* Keep this form with your ledger.

2. Count all the money in your **Business Money Keeper**. Check to make sure the total amount of money in your **Business Money Keeper** matches the **Balance** in your ledger. <u>These totals must be the same.</u>

If the totals are not the same, look for a mistake in your ledger and recount your money. If you cannot find your mistake, you may need help.

3. If you need your teacher to help find your mistake, take these two things to class:

    A. An up-to-date ledger.

    B. A piece of paper with the total amount you have in your **Business Money Keeper**.

In Lesson 27, you will divide your business money into your *JOEYS* Treasure Keepers.

Do NOT bring your money to class!

Kingdom Keys

Key to the Lesson

I will be a financial winner if I make good choices and become thrifty!

Key Ideas

Clue to the Code
KCKs are financial winners because they *make do.*

Character Code
Become Thrifty

Treasure of the Kingdom
KCKs make good choices when they spend their money.

Key Terms

thrifty (**thrif**-tē) carefully using money and other resources

utilities (ū-**til**-i-tēs) services that are provided to the public

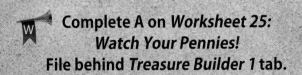
Complete A on *Worksheet 25:*
Watch Your Pennies!
File behind *Treasure Builder 1* tab.

Be thrifty!
Turn off the lights.

CONGRATULATIONS

You may place your Level Twenty-five reward on the KCK Treasure Map.

Bonus Code Work

1. Many quotes have been made about money. Research and find a quote you like. Write it, tell who said it, and explain why you like it. You can ask your mentor or parent for help.

2. Think of ways your family *makes do*. Make a Thrifty Tips poster. Share it with your class.

3. Ask your parent or teacher for permission to use the internet to research ways to be thrifty. Write your top three favorites, and share them with someone.

4. Look for coupons in the newspaper, in store flyers, or online. Start collecting coupons for your family to use.

Thrifty Tips from the Hilder Home

#1: We only go to the movies on Wednesday because it is Half Price Night. Fun!

#2: We treat ourselves to pizza on Monday nights because it is Buy One Get One Free at Papa's Pizza. Yum!

5. Ask older adults to give you ideas of how to *make do*. Make a list, or draw a picture.

Lesson 26

What Did You Say?

Proclamation

I will encourage others by listening to them and saying good things.

KCKs, you encourage others when you say nice things. What are some things people say to you that make you feel good?

- **You're a great friend.**
- **You make me happy.**
- **I have fun when we're together.**
- **I like to talk to you because you listen.**

Now, stand and repeat the *Proclamation*.

Check Your Path

Begin *Worksheet 26: What Did You Say?*

Quest for the Clue

Have you ever talked with a friend using a can and string telephone? Have you ever written a note? Have you ever waved to someone? If you have, you practiced the art of **communication** (kuh-mū-ni-**kā**-shun). Communication is the act of using words, sounds, signs, or actions to give or exchange information.

Since the beginning of time, different types of communication have been used. Can you guess the first way people communicated? They certainly did not text!

Over the years, changes in communication have made the world more interdependent. How? Inventions have made it easier for the United States and other countries to trade. For example, the internet made it simpler for people to buy and sell across the globe.

Look at the timeline on the next page. What do you think is the most important invention that changed the way people communicate?

Changes in Communication

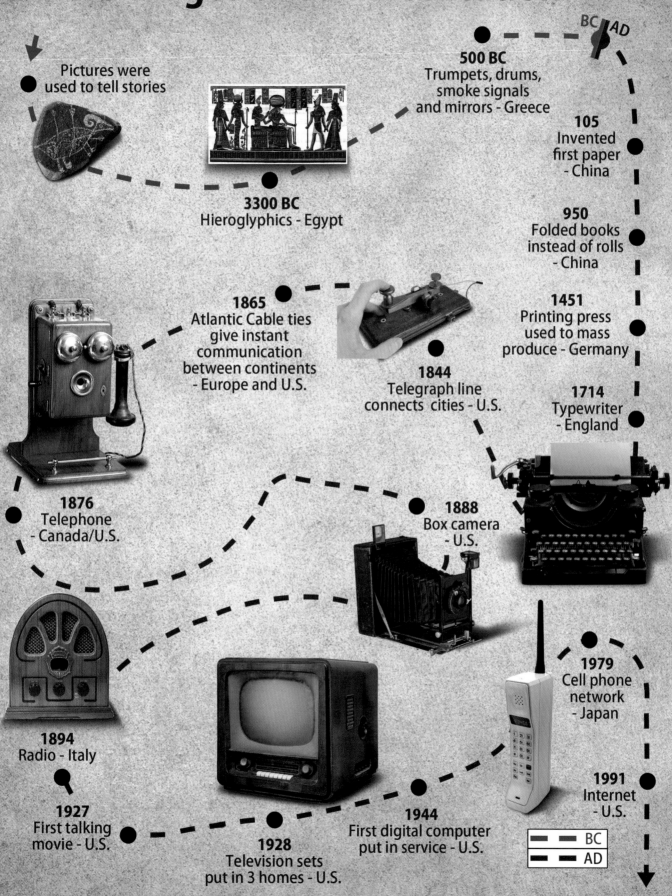

BC | AD

Pictures were used to tell stories

500 BC
Trumpets, drums, smoke signals and mirrors - Greece

105
Invented first paper - China

3300 BC
Hieroglyphics - Egypt

950
Folded books instead of rolls - China

1865
Atlantic Cable ties give instant communication between continents - Europe and U.S.

1451
Printing press used to mass produce - Germany

1844
Telegraph line connects cities - U.S.

1714
Typewriter - England

1876
Telephone - Canada/U.S.

1888
Box camera - U.S.

1979
Cell phone network - Japan

1894
Radio - Italy

1991
Internet - U.S.

1927
First talking movie - U.S.

1944
First digital computer put in service - U.S.

1928
Television sets put in 3 homes - U.S.

BC
AD

✦— What Did You Say? —✦

From: *Aunt Jimmi*

Dear Kingdom Code Kids,

I want to tell you how changes in communication affected our business.

When Johnny first started the company in 1974, he had customers in many states. To make a sale, he got in his truck, visited the customers, and wrote down their orders. Then he drove around until he found a telephone booth, put money in the telephone, and read the order to someone back at the office. After this, the rivets could be shipped.

During our first years in business, our customers did not use email, cell phones, or the internet. The only way they could learn about new rivets or tools was to read about them, hear about them over the phone, or see someone else using them. No internet! No cell phones! No quick way to get information back and forth to each other.

As time passed, the communication industry exploded. Talk about exciting! Advances in communication have totally changed the way we do business today. Can you imagine what changes will take place in the next fifty years? You may even be a great inventor who makes a difference in people's lives.

Yours truly,
Aunt Jimmi

Changes in communication make it easier for you to contact potential customers and build your business.

You will communicate with your customers, friends, and family all your life. Whether you speak or write, it is important to always be a good communicator (kuh-**mū**-ni-kā-ter).

Being a good communicator means you:

• **Describe your ideas clearly.**

• **Listen carefully.**

• **Ask questions if you do not understand.**

Some people are shy, and find it hard to speak up. Do you remember how Aunt Jimmi felt when she began to make sales calls? She was terrified. What did she do to get over her fear? She practiced making calls until she gained confidence. With every call, Aunt Jimmi learned to communicate better. You can too.

 If you are shy, ask Jesus to give you confidence.

Communication gives you the power to...

- **Solve problems.**
- **Make new friends.**
- **Supply your needs and wants.**
- **Sell to potential customers.**

Great communication can help your business grow. How? With sales calls and advertising, you can make a great first impression to potential customers. Be sure to choose your words carefully, speak clearly, and write neatly. These three communication skills will help you gain confidence as you communicate with others.

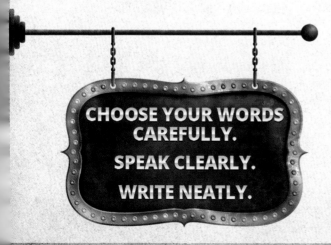

CHOOSE YOUR WORDS CAREFULLY.

SPEAK CLEARLY.

WRITE NEATLY.

✦ Action Time ✦

Remember, communication is shown with words, sounds, signs, and actions.

Create and perform two skits showing different ways to communicate in the same situation. First, show someone with a bad attitude. Then, give the same skit showing someone with a good attitude.

You have found the **Clue**.

🔍 **Learning to communicate well helps KCKs build their businesses and gain confidence.**

🎺 1. Complete *Activity 39: Communication Then and Now.*

Code of Honor

> When you talk, don't say anything bad. But say the good things that people need — whatever will help them grow stronger. Then what you say will be a blessing to those who hear you... Be kind and loving to each other. Forgive each other the same as God forgave you through Christ.
>
> — Ephesians 4:29, 32 ERV

Do you know how to get rid of mean word rocks from your life?

Show Honor

You show honor to others with the words you say. Choose your words carefully. When you hurt someone with words, it takes a long time to get over the pain. In fact, some people do not know how to get past the unkind or cruel words said to them. They carry the mean words around like heavy rocks in a backpack.

DROP THEM AND WALK AWAY...

FAR Away!

Forgive the person who said the mean words to you.

Ask God to remove the mean words from your mind.

Replace the mean words with good thoughts about the situation.

HAVE A GOOD ATTITUDE.

Kingdom Code Kids Think Differently!

We show honor with our words, and forgive those who say mean things.

KCKs, God made you special. No matter what words may be said about you, know in your heart...

YOU ARE AMAZING!

You have talent and skills to use for God's Kingdom, so never let mean words change the way you feel about yourself. Never let someone's words cause you to make a bad decision either. Remember...

**You Are a
Valuable Knight
in the Army of God.**

1. When you are communicating, how can you show honor with your words, head, face, eyes, shoulders, and sounds?

2. There are many ways to show honor when you communicate. For example, if an older person cannot hear well, you may need to speak slower or louder. Give different ways of showing respect and honor to:

   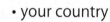

   - God
   - teachers
   - customers
   - police
   - firemen
   - parents
   - friends
   - your country

3. Be a blessing to others with your words. Make a list of good things you can say that will encourage others.

Treasure Seeking

How many times have you heard?

I didn't know!

Nobody told me!

Whether you are dealing with friends, family, or customers, it is important to keep people informed. Call, text, email, or write a note.

Gone to mow grass at Mr. Hall's house.

When you fail to communicate or get back with someone who is expecting an answer, you have let the *lines of communication* break down. People are much happier and work goes more smoothly when all the facts are known and everyone is informed.

Knights, if you learn to communicate well, you will be a winner!

Challenge!

Show honor when you communicate.

• **Be polite.**

• **Ask questions to understand.**

• **Get and give correct information.**

• **Say "Please" and "Thank you".**

These are communication skills that will help you the rest of your life.

Another communication skill you can practice is being **courteous** (**kur**-tē-us). Courteous means to show respect and be polite. Be courteous even when someone is rude to you. Wow! Sometimes, that is really hard to do, but it is **The Kingdom Code** way.

One way to show honor and be courteous is to *listen* to what others are saying.

Listening is part of communicating well.

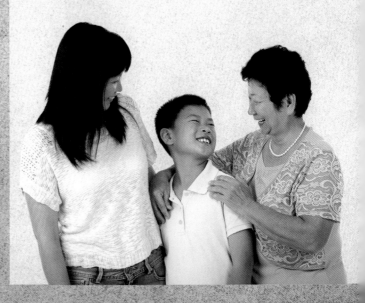

KCKs, listen to understand what your customers really need and want. If you do not give your total attention to what the customer says, you might work hard, but still fail to do what the customer wants. For example, pretend your customer tells you to clean up the area along the fence. You work very hard pulling out the tall weeds and cutting everything down. You are surprised when the customer is mad. He had little trees along the fence, but did not make it clear to leave the trees and pull only the weeds. Before starting a job, it is important to understand what the customer wants. Be a great listener. Ask questions until you know what to do.

Communication wins favor!

Be honest and tell others how you feel, but give only constructive criticism. For example, pretend a friend asks you, "Do you like my logo?" If you do not like it, do not just say, "No!" Give some ideas to make it better instead of hurting the person's feelings. Communicating well means being honest and clear, but not being mean to anyone.

Every time you have the chance, bless others by using kind words.

You have found the Treasure.

Good communication wins favor, blesses others, and leads to success.

On Your Own

A 1. In Lesson 27, you divide the money from your **Business Money Keeper**, and put it into your *JOEYS* Treasure Keepers.

• Update your ledger.

• Be sure your ledger **Balance** is the same as the total amount of money in your **Business Money Keeper**.

• Write this total on a piece of paper, and bring this paper to class.

Remember: _Do not take your money to class!_

2. Prepare a presentation about your Treasure Builder for Lesson 27 to share with your class. Be sure to include the following:

• **Describe your business.**

• **Give personal experiences.**

• **Show pictures or drawings.**

• **Write comments from customers.**

Kingdom Keys

Key to the Lesson

My key to success is to honor others through good communication.

Key Ideas

Clue to the Code
Learning to communicate well helps **KCKs** build their businesses and gain confidence.

Character Code
Show Honor

Treasure of the Kingdom
Good communication wins favor, blesses others, and leads to success.

Key Terms

communication (kuh-mū-ni-**kā**-shun) the act of using words, sounds, signs, or actions to give or exchange information

courteous (**kur**-tē-us) to show respect and be polite

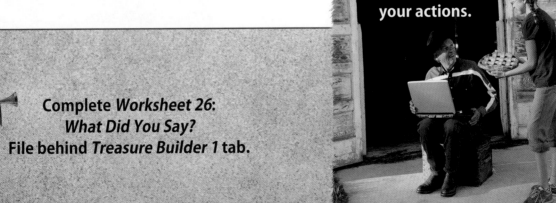

Honor others with your actions.

W Complete *Worksheet 26:*
What Did You Say?
File behind *Treasure Builder 1* tab.

CONGRATULATIONS

You may place your Level Twenty-six reward on the KCK Treasure Map.

Bonus Code Work

1. Choose a communication event from the timeline in the lesson. Give an example of how this event influenced the world economy.

2. Be very creative. Use a different way to communicate than you normally do. For example: Make a telephone using two cans and a string, or mail a letter to a friend.

3. Practice your Key Terms. Use your flash cards.

4. Get together with your friends and write a newspaper story about an invention that helps people communicate. You can invent your own, or pretend this is the first time the invention has been presented to the world.

5. Find a Bible verse about showing honor, such as Exodus 20:12. Write it, memorize it, and share it with someone.

Lesson 27

An Honest Review

Proclamation

I will be wise and look ahead. I will face facts and not be foolish.

KCKs, your whole future is ahead of you. It will be shaped by the choices you make and the code by which you live. Use common sense as you live your life for Christ. Now, stand and repeat the *Proclamation*. While standing, put on the Armor of God.

Check Your Path

Begin *Worksheet 27: An Honest Review.*

Quest for the Clue

Bring out the balloons and throw the confetti!

You have so much to be excited about!

With all the **Clues** you followed and the **Treasures** you found, you took a risk and built a Treasure Builder. Along the way, you gained experience and became an entrepreneur.

You followed the path of **The Kingdom Code.**

You learned how to Make and Manage Money... God's Way!

Keys to The Kingdom Code

The Kingdom Code pathway
leads you to success and happiness.

- I can own a business in a free enterprise system.

- I am an entrepreneur who has the courage to take risks and seek advice.

- I can write a business plan and create a marketing strategy.

- I choose to be organized.

- I enjoy learning.

- I follow the KCK Sales Code when I make sales calls.

- I am building a good reputation by working hard and treating others like I want to be treated.

- I plan ahead and save for my future.

- I can budget money wisely with the KCK Budget.

- I reach my goals because I am aware of my strengths.

- I know, use, and share my talents.

- I seek wisdom to solve problems and make good choices.

- I choose to work, be independent, and keep my freedom.

- I know Jesus is my source of strength.

- I know how to *make do* by using available resources.

- I know that every choice I make has a consequence.

A Kingdom Code Kid Thinks Differently!

I choose to be content with what I have.

I save for my education to fulfill my dreams.

I know God is with me and helps me be bold.

I know the importance of a mentor.

I never promise something I cannot do.

I have courage to ask for help.

I face the future with an expectant heart.

I take initiative and do more than what is expected.

I will make a difference in the world!

⚜ Share Your Thoughts ⚜

Talk about things you have learned this year that will help you in the future.

1. What skills and talents did you discover?

2. Share what you learned about managing a business.

3. Why should you set goals?

4. Share what you learned about impulse buying and being thrifty.

5. Why is it important to work hard so you can be independent?

6. What have you learned that will help you the most as you get older?

7. How can choices you make now affect your life and your future?

You have found another Clue.

🔍 **KCKs are successful because they follow The Kingdom Code.**

Code of Honor

From: *Aunt Jimmi*

Dear Kingdom Code Kids,

I've been thinking about some things my parents taught me about being honest.

Mother always said, "If you tell the truth, you never have to remember what you said!" She knew if I told a lie, I could forget what I said. Then later, someone would uncover the truth.

Knights, if people can't trust what you say, they will not want to do business with you or be your friend.

My dad felt honesty should be shown in the way you act. He told me a thousand times, "If you don't have principles, you are not worth much!" To him, principles were being honest and treating people the way he wanted to be treated and respected.

My parents are both in heaven now, but they showed me what it meant to be honest in both words and actions. I want you to have integrity too. You can do this every day of your life!

Always be a shining light to others when you work or play. It is <u>The Kingdom Code</u> way.

I am very proud of what you have done so far.

God be with you!
Aunt Jimmi

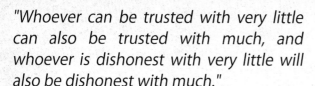

"Whoever can be trusted with very little can also be trusted with much, and whoever is dishonest with very little will also be dishonest with much."

— Luke 16:10 NIV

Be Honest

Sometimes it is hard to look at yourself honestly. It is much easier to look at what others do. In fact, it is not much fun to look at your own mistakes, but that is the way to learn and improve. To admit that you are doing something wrong takes a lot of courage.

Knights, it is time to take a look at your Treasure Builder and be very honest.

Ask yourself, "Do I enjoy my business?"

After you know the answer, you have two **options** (**op**-shunz). Options are choices. You can continue your service business, or you can choose to start a new business.

Do Not Forget!

Ask God for discernment to help you choose wisely.

Knights, you will soon be dividing the money in your **Business Money Keeper**.

You may start your next business very soon or expand the business you have now. Either way, you need to save all the money you put into your *Y Treasure Keeper*.

The money in your *Y Treasure Keeper* will be used to begin a new **Treasure Builder 2**, or expand your **Treasure Builder 1**. You can decide later how much money you want to invest. It is your choice.

Choose wisely!

KCKs, do you have a special place to keep your *Treasure Keepers*?

Your money needs to be in a safe place. If you cannot think of a safe place to keep your money, ask someone you trust for ideas.

The day has arrived!
A special event is about to take place.

Treasure Seeking

It is time to transfer your money from your **Business Money Keeper** into your *JOEYS Treasure Keepers*.

J is for ***Jesus***.
Honor the Lord with your money.

O is for *Others*.
It is fun to share your money with others.

E is for *Education*.
Now is the time to save for the education you will need later.

Y is for *You*.
All the money in the *Y Treasure Keeper* can be used for your **Treasure Builder 2.**

S is for *Savings*.
Knights, long-term savings is paying yourself in advance, so you will have it later. Keep emergency savings for something you do not expect to happen.

Do you remember the percent that goes into each *Treasure Keeper*?

 *J* = 10%

 *O* = 5%

 *E* = 10%

 Y = 60%

 *S* = 15%

Your **Business Money Keeper** will soon be empty. To refill it, keep your business going or start a new one quickly.

Great job, KCKs!

You are on a new quest
to use your *JOEYS* Treasure Keepers.

Knights, the **Treasure** has been found.

KCKs manage money by using
***JOEYS* Treasure Keepers.**

On Your Own

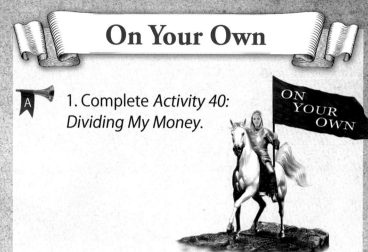

1. Complete *Activity 40: Dividing My Money.*

Now, use the **KCK Budget** by dividing your business money and filling your *JOEYS Treasure Keepers.*

2. After giving your presentation, let's write Aunt Jimmi a letter. She would enjoy hearing from you. You can tell her about your business, and include some of the following:

- What did you like most about building your business?

- Describe a fun business experience.

- What part of the **KCK Budget** are you excited about?

- What hidden gifts or talents did you discover that you can share with others?

- Which Character Code has helped you succeed the most?

- What goals have you set for your future education and career?

- Share what you liked best about **The Kingdom Code**.

Kingdom Keys

Key to the Lesson

I am honest as I manage my money and follow The Kingdom Code.

Key Ideas

Clue to the Code
KCKs are successful because they follow **The Kingdom Code**.

Character Code
Be Honest

Treasure of the Kingdom
KCKs manage money by using *JOEYS* *Treasure Keepers*.

Key Terms

options (**op**-shunz) choices

We are successful KCKs!

Complete *Worksheet 27: An Honest Review*.
File behind *Treasure Builder 1* tab.

CONGRATULATIONS

You have earned your Level Twenty-seven reward on the KCK Treasure Map.

Bonus Code Work

1. Write a thank you note to your mentor or any other person who has helped you create a successful service business.

2. If you are good with computers, ask your parents or teacher for permission to create a website for your service business. Share the website with your customers and friends. Keep your website updated with information about your business.

advertising (**ad**-ver-tī-zing) making people aware of an event, service, or product

analyze (**an**-uh-līz) to study something carefully

appointment (uh-**point**-munt) a plan to be somewhere at a set time and date

appropriate (uh-**prō**-prē-it) right for the time

budget (**buj**-it) a plan used to decide how money will be spent

business plan (**biz**-nis) (plan) a written plan telling how to start and manage a business

calculate (**kal**-kyuh-lāt) to solve a problem by using math

capital (**kap**-i-tl) money or property used in a business

capitalism (**ka**-pi-tl-iz-um) a system where the people, not the government, have the right to start, own, and manage a business to make money

career (kuh-**reer**) the lifework a person chooses to earn a living

Christianity (kris-chē-**an**-i-tē) the religion which teaches and believes Jesus is the Son of God and the Savior of the world

commerce (**kom**-ers) business or trade

communication (kuh-mū-ni-**kā**-shun) the act of using words, sounds, signs, or actions to give or exchange information

compete (kum-**pēt**) to try to get or win something that someone else is also trying to get or win

confidence (**kon**-fi-dents) believing you can succeed

consequence (**kon**-si-kwens) something that happens because of an action

constructive criticism (kun-**struk**-tiv) (**krit**-uh-siz-um) giving ideas to help others improve

consumer (kun-**soo**-mer) a person who buys goods or services

content (kun-**tent**) being happy with what you have

courteous (**kur**-tē-us) to show respect and be polite

creativity (krē-ā-**tiv**-i-tē) making new things or coming up with new ideas

currency (**kur**-uhn-sē) any form of money used for exchange

data (**dā**-tuh) facts or information, usually used to study or plan something

debt (det) money you owe

demand (di-**mand**) the desire and ability to buy goods or services

dependent (dih-**pen**-dunt) to be under the control of another; to rely on someone or something else

deposit (dih-**poz**-it) 1. (verb) to put money in a bank account; 2. (noun) an amount of money put in a bank account

determination (di-tur-muh-**nā**-shun) not giving up

diligence (**dil**-i-juns) working with all the might and power you can give

discernment (dih-**surn**-munt) the ability to know, understand, and judge correctly

earnings (**ur**-ningz) money received for work or services

economics (ek-uh-**nom**-iks) the study of people using their time, talents, and money to produce, buy, and sell goods and services

economy (ē-**kon**-uh-mē) the way goods and services are made, sold, and bought in an area

emotional appeal (ē-**mō**-shuh-nl) (uh-**pēl**) advertising with the focus on feelings

emotions (ē-**mō**-shunz) strong feelings inside you

entitlement (en-**tī**-tl-munt) a feeling or belief that you deserve to be given something

entrepreneur (ahn-truh-pruh-**noor**) a person who takes a risk to start and manage a business

entry (**en**-trē) a written record in a ledger that gives important details about a transaction

evaluate (ih-**val**-yū-āt) carefully judge the value or condition of something

expectant (ik-**spek**-tunt) to believe or act like something good is going to happen

expense (ik-**spens**) money spent

financial (fi-**nan**-shul) anything that has to do with money

financial responsibility (fi-**nan**-shul) (rē-spon-suh-**bil**-i-tē) a debt or a bill

financial security (fi-**nan**-shul) (si-**kyoor**-i-tē) having enough money for your needs now and for the future

financially responsible (fi-**nan**-shuh-lē) (rē-**spon**-suh-bul) spending money wisely, paying what you owe, not spending more than you can afford

first impression (furst) (im-**presh**-un) what people think about another person the first time they meet

fixed expense (fikst) (ik-**spens**) a business cost which usually does not change

free enterprise (frē) (**en**-ter-prīz) a system where private businesses compete with each other with little control by the government

generosity (jen-uh-**ros**-i-tē) the act of giving something of value to someone else

gross income (grōs) (**in**-kum) the total amount of money received from sales and services

historical fiction (hi-**stor**-i-kul) (**fik**-shun) imaginary stories about facts, events, or people from the past

immigrants (**im**-i-grents) people who leave one country to make a new home in another country

impulse buying (**im**-puls) (**bī**-ing) purchasing something without planning or thinking it through

income (**in**-kum) money received

independent (in-di-**pen**-dunt) to be free; rely on oneself; to think or act for oneself

initiative (ih-**nish**-uh-tiv) knowing what needs to be done and doing it

Integrity (in-**teg**-ri-tē) being honest, truthful, trustworthy, and doing what is right

interdependent (in-ter-di-**pen**-dunt) people or things that depend on each other

interest rate (**in**-ter-ist) (rāt) the amount of money charged or paid for using money

invest (in-**vest**) to put money into something that could bring back a financial profit

ledger (**lej**-er) a record of the money a business has received or spent

logo (**lō**-gō) the symbol of a business

loss (los) when a business has more expenses than income

market (**mar**-kit) anywhere buying and selling can happen

marketing strategy (**mar**-ki-ting) (**strat**-i-jē) a plan to tell consumers about a service or product

mentor (**men**-tawr) a trusted person who gives advice and teaches others

needs (nēdz) things required to help a person survive

net income (net) (**in**-kum) the difference between gross income and expenses

occupation (ock-yuh-**pā**-shun) the work a person does to earn a living

opportunity (op-er-**too**-ni-tē) a chance to do something

options (**op**-shunz) choices

percent (per-**sent**) one part in a hundred (1/100 or 1%)

perseverance (pur-suh-**veer**-uns) to continue trying even if it is difficult

persuasive (per-**swā**-siv) being able to convince people to do or believe something

pride (prīd) a feeling of happiness that comes from doing something well

principles (**prin**-suh-pulz) rules and beliefs which guide your thoughts, words, and actions

proclamation (prok-luh-**mā**-shun) an important statement said out loud

professional (pruh-**fesh**-uh-nl) a person who is an expert in his or her work

profit (**prah**-fit) when a business has more income than expenses

receipt (ri-**sēt**) a written record showing something given and received

reputation (rep-yū-**tā**-shun) what others believe and think about another person

resource (**rē**-sors) an available supply to be used when needed

resourceful (rē-**sōrs**-ful) finding clever ways to meet needs and wants

revelation (rev-uh-**lā**-shun) a new idea or greater understanding

security (si-**kyoor**-i-tē) the feeling of being safe

self-control (self) (kun-**trōl**) the ability to stop yourself from doing things you want to do, but might not be the best for you

sole proprietorship (sōl) (pruh-**pri**-i-ter-ship) a business which is owned and run by one person

solution (suh-**loo**-shun) an answer to a problem

spiritual gift (**spir**-i-choo-ul) (gift) a special ability given by God

steward (**stoo**-erd) a person who takes care of something that belongs to someone else

strategy (**strat**-i-jē) a plan to reach a goal

summary (**sum**-uh-rē) a short review giving the main points of something

supply (suh-**plī**) the amount of goods or services available to buy

survey (**sur**-vā) an activity to find what people think about something

talent (**tal**-unt) a special ability to do something very well

taxes (**taks**-iz) required payments of money to state or federal governments

thrifty (**thrif**-tē) carefully using money and other resources

tithe (tīth) an offering for God, usually one tenth

transaction (tran-**zak**-shun) an event where money is transferred

trend (trind) a direction something goes or changes

utilities (ū-**til**-i-tēs) services that are provided to the public

variable expense (**vair**-ē-uh-bul) (ik-**spens**) a business cost which can change

wants (wawnts) things a person desires but does not need to survive

withdraw (with-**draw**) to remove money from a bank account

Word definitions have been simplified to promote easier understanding. Consult a dictionary for more precise definitions.

Bibliography

Lesson 2
Bellis, Mary. "John Deere - Invented a Better Plow." *About.com Inventors*. About.com, 17 June 2015. Web. 29 Dec. 2015. (pp. 12, 13.)

"How Does the US Free Enterprise System Work?" *Free Enterprise*. The Social Studies Help Center, n.d. Web. 16 Apr. 2014. (p. 14.)

"John Deere's Plow." *Story of the John Deere Plow*. Deere & Company, 2014. Web. 16 Apr. 2014. (pp. 12, 13.)

Lesson 3
Alchin, Linda. "Railroads in the 1800s." : *History for Kids* ***. Siteseen Ltd., Sept. 2015. Web. 30 Dec. 2015. (pp. 24, 25.)

Anderson, H. Allen. "GOODNIGHT, CHARLES." *ANDERSON, H. ALLEN*. Texas State Historical Association, n.d. Web. 31 Dec. 2015.

"History of the JA, The Ritchie Family and the JA Family." *JA Ranch*. N.p., n.d. Web. 16 Apr. 2014. (pp. 20-24.)

"Law of Supply and Demand." *The Free Dictionary*. Farlex, 2003-2015. Web. 30 Dec. 2015. (p. 21.)

"Law Of Supply And Demand Definition | *Investopedia*." Investopedia. Investopedia, LLC., 19 May 2010. Web. 30 Dec. 2015. (p. 21.)

Lesson 5
John, Steven. "The World's Top 5 Most Watched Sporting Events." *The World's Top 5 Most Watched Sporting Events*. Talent Submissions, 2015. Web. 30 Dec. 2015. (p. 38.)

Lesson 6
"Joan of Arc." *History.com*. A&E Television Networks, 2009. Web. 15 Apr. 2015. (p. 49.)

Lesson 13
Anderson, Kelly. "The Complete History of the Piggy Bank." *Drupal 7 (http://drupal.org)*. N.p., n.d. Web. 7 May 2014. (pp. 106, 107.)

Lesson 14
"ExplorePAHistory.com - Image." *ExplorePAHistory.com - Image*. Pennsylvania State Archives, n.d. Web. 30 Dec. 2015. (p. 114.)

"Henry John Heinz: A Man of Uncommon Vision." - *History*. H.J. Heinz Company, n.d. Web. 18 May 2014. (pp. 113, 114.)

Note: Special thanks to Sally Stodolsky and Sabrina J. Hudson of the H.J. Heinz Company for their assistance securing permission to publish the historical fiction about H.J. Heinz and images. (case #003936250A)

Lesson 15
"Thomas Edison." *Thomas Edison - Edison Innovation Foundation*. Edison Innovation Foundation, 2014. Web. 30 Dec. 2015. (pp. 120-122.)

"Thomas Edison Lightbulb." *Thomas Edison Muckers RSS*. Edison Innovation Foundation, 20 Feb. 2011. Web. 30 Dec. 2015. (pp. 120-122.)

Lesson 18
McGinnity, B. L., J. Seymour-Ford, and K. J. Andries. "Anne Sullivan." *Perkins School for the Blind*. Perkins School for the Blind, 2004. Web. 30 Dec. 2015. (pp. 148, 149.)

McGinnity, B. L., J. Seymour-Ford, and K. J. Andries. "Helen Keller FAQ." *Perkins School for the Blind*. Perkins School for the Blind, 2004. Web. 30 Dec. 2015. (pp. 148, 149.)

Note: Special thanks to Jan Seymour-Ford, research librarian at Perkins School for the Blind, for her help securing information and images for this lesson.

Lesson 19
Knox, Dr. E. L. Skip. "Europe in the Middle Ages: Banks and Money." *Currency and Banking in the Late Middle Ages*. Boise State University, n.d. Web. 27 July 2014. (pp. 152, 153.)

"The Wells Fargo Treasure Box." *The Wells Fargo Stagecoach*. Wells Fargo Company, 199902014. Web. 2 Aug. 2014. (pp. 155, 156.)

Lesson 21
Ashliman, D. L. "The Pied Piper of Hameln." *Pied Piper of Hameln*. N.p., 1999-2013. Web. 30 Dec. 2015. (pp. 168, 169.)

Lesson 22
De León, Arnoldo. "MEXICAN TEXAS." *A Digital Gateway to Texas History*. Texas State Historical Association, 15 June 2010. Web. 5 Aug. 2014. (pp. 176-183.)

Dethloff, Henry C., and Garry L. Nall. "AGRICULTURE." *A Digital Gateway to Texas History*. Texas State Historical Association, 4 Sept. 2013. Web. 30 Dec. 2015. (pp. 176-183.)

Spain, Charles A., Jr. "FLAGS OF TEXAS." *Handbook of Texas Online*. Texas State Historical Association, 12 June 2010. Web. 18 July 2014. (pp. 178-181.)

TBH Web Team. "How Many Ways Can You Use a Buffalo?" *KIDS Only?* - Fun Stuff To Do. Texas Beyond History, 1 Oct. 2001. Web. 18 July 2014. (p. 177.)

The Texas Historical Commission. "Six Flags Over Texas." *Texas Register 22* (1997): 5959-967. Texas Register. Web. 18 July 2014. (pp. 178-181.)

Bredeson, Carmen. *Texas*. New York: Benchmark, 1997. 55-57. Print. (pp. 176-183.)

Somervill, Barbara A. *Texas*. New York: Scholastic, 2008. 24+. Print. (pp. 176-183.)

Teitelbaum, Michael. *Texas, 1527-1836*. Washington, D.C.: National Geographic Society, 2005. 79+. Print. (pp. 176-183.)

Turner, Robyn. *Texas Traditions: The Culture of the Lone Star State*. Boston: Little, Brown, 1996. 10+. Print. (pp. 176-183.)

Lesson 25
"Money Quotes." *Money Quotes*. Famous Quotes and Authors.com, 2011. Web. 21 May 2014.

Lesson 26
Fang, Irving. "Communication Timeline." Timeline of Communication History (1995-1996): n. p. *COMMUNICATION TIMELINE.doc*. School of Journalism and Mass Communication. Web. 23 July 2015. (p. 211.)

"TIMELINE - Major Events in the History of Mass Communications." *TIMELINE*. Office of Curriculum & Instruction/Indiana Department of Education, 2008. Web. 23 July 2015. (p. 211.)

Note: Some internet sites, especially websites of government agencies, can be good sources of information; but you should consult them carefully and only with your parent's permission. We make no guarantees about the reliability or propriety of everything on all the websites cited in this work or of the links posted on those websites to other sites.

Credits

Used by permission: Alyssa Maisano, photographer, www.alyssamaisanophotography.com (models on front cover.)

Used by permission: Kymberly Marshall, photographer (pp. 2, 127, 159.)

Used by permission: Cassandra Dorman, www.theunpluggedfamily.com, paper mache piggy banks (p. 109.)

Library of Congress, Prince & Photographs Division, John C. H. Grabill Collection, [reproduction number, e.g., [LC-USZ62-12345], photo of Wells Fargo Express Co. Deadwood Treasure Wagon and Guards, S.D. 1890. (p. 155.)

Used by permission: Robert Warren, Museum of Illinois, photo of reproduction of 1837 John Deere steel-blade plow. (p. 12.)

Used by permission: Doug Stremel, photographer, www.dougstremel.com, longhorn cattle (pp. 20, 21, 47.)
Note: Special thanks to Gwen Hoy of Flint Hills Flying W Ranch, Kansas, www.flinthillsflyingw.com, who assisted in securing permissions and images of longhorn cattle. (pp. 20, 21, 47.)

Used by permission: H.J. Heinz Company, Pittsburg, Pennsylvania. (case #003936250A) (pp. 113, 114.)

Used by permission: "Image Gallery." *Perkins School for the Blind Archives*. Perkins School for the Blind, n.d. Web. 29 Dec. 2015. (pp. 148, 149.) Note: Special thanks to the research librarians who helped obtain these images.

Permission granted by the following individuals whose pictures appear in the curriculum:
Khloe Bolander
Micah and Keira Brush
Chandon Burton
John and MaKenzie Byler
Logan Daniels
Billie Earle
Christy, Alyssa, Baylis, Madilyn, and Savannah Earle
Katelyn and Kylie Earle
Morgan and Mikayla Earle
Isaiah Edwards
Brennan, Caden, and Graham Forsythe
Jax Garner
Donna Forsythe
Moritz and Philip Hammerstädt
Gene and Jack Herrmann
Wyatt and Aaron Hilder
Jang Hyeon Lee, Master Taekwondo Instructor, www.jtigers.com/j/index.php?mid=page_OTPs19
Mckenzie and Mia Miranda
Mark Zauss, medieval icon trumpeter, www.bandsourceproductions.com/

J&J Music, J. Marshall, www.jandjmusicokc.com, song and lyrics (p. 11.)

Gratitude is given to the following people who graciously shared their expertise and knowledge to enrich and make the curriculum possible: Ronald Johnson, Ph D; Moose Stovall, CPA, PFC; Sharan Northrupp; Merlene Byler, Administrator - Faith Academy Bellville; Ken Cummins; Heather Jane Link; Andrea Cruz; Cathy Abercrombie; Heather Hermann; and Kimberly Zahorik.

Special thanks to my prayer warriors Beth Alves, Kate Forsythe, Billie Earle, Barbie Breathitt, Ruthanne Garlock, Marcy Malkey, Kay Curtis, and Myra Harbin, plus all the women who attended the women's retreats. They prayed **The Kingdom Code** curriculum into existence and continue to pray for it and the lives it will influence.

A

advertise 40, 42, 51, 59, 169-73, 201
advertising 39-44, 55, 62, 134, 170, 173-75, 190, 213
advertisement(s) 169-175
analyze 133, 136
appointment 53-54, 57-58, 62, 67, 69, 75, 83, 91, 99, 115, 163
appropriate 82, 84
Armor of God 3-4, 9-10, 12, 20, 28, 47, 52, 60, 127, 152, 220

B

balance 65-67, 91, 99, 107
bill(s) 5-6, 9, 128, 146, 187, 205
budget 71-74, 76-77, 82, 83, 89, 98, 102-4, 107, 117, 167, 221, 227
business plan 20, 28-31, 33-36, 38, 42-43, 45, 119, 123, 145, 221
Business Money Keeper 7, 57, 63-66, 71, 83, 89, 91, 95, 98-99, 107, 135, 207, 217, 225-27

C

calculate 145-47, 150
capital 41, 44, 66, 99, 225, 227
capitalism 14-16, 18, 21, 182, 196
career 8-92, 139, 142, 188, 196

Christianity 178, 184
Certificate of Deposit (CD) 154-55
commerce 179, 183-4
communicate 149, 212-13, 215-16, 218-19
communication 210, 212-13, 216-19
communicator 212
compete 14-15, 18, 38, 41
competition 14, 38-41, 44, 51
confidence 53, 55, 58, 110, 160, 164-5, 212-13, 218, 221
consequence(s) 138, 142-3, 221
constructive criticism 46, 50, 217
consumer(s) 32, 35, 39-40, 44, 96, 173, 175, 190, 195
content 104-05, 107-10, 196
courteous 216, 218
creativity 114, 116, 120
currency 152-53, 158

D

data 132-37, 161
debt(s) 5-6, 9
Deere, John 12-13, 19
demand 21-22, 26-27, 47- 48, 51
dependent 187-89, 192, 194-96
deposit(s) 153-54, 156, 158
determination 114-16, 120
diligence 90, 92
discernment 170-71, 173-74, 225

E

earning(s) 6, 57, 145-46, 150, 195, 198
economics 2, 5, 9-10, 21, 32, 71
economy 13-14, 18-19, 25, 176-77, 179-81, 183-84, 219
Edison, Thomas 120-22
emotional appeal 170, 173-74, 190
emotion(s) 169-71, 173-75, 202
entitlement 194-96, 200
entrepreneur(s) 12-13, 16, 18, 20, 22-23, 25-27, 41, 62, 117, 139, 179, 181, 196, 220-21
entry 65-68
evaluate 118-20, 122-25
evaluation 46, 119, 123
evaluation card 46
expectant 120-21, 124, 164, 188
expense(s) 61, 64-66, 68, 128, 130, 132-34, 145-47, 150, 207

F

face-to-face sales 56
financial 40, 44, 99-100, 157-58, 203-04, 208
financial plan 30, 40-41, 43-44
financial responsibility 5-6, 9
financial security 72, 76
financially responsible 5-6, 8-9, 62, 64, 71, 158, 198
first impression 55, 58, 112-13, 213
fixed expense 128, 132, 136
free enterprise 14-16, 18, 23, 190, 196, 221

My KCK
Sales Code

1. My hair, hands, body, and teeth are clean.

2. I look into the other person's eyes when we talk to each other.

3. I have a firm but kind handshake.

4. My clothes and shoes are neat and clean so anyone is comfortable talking to me.

5. I smile and say, "Please" and "Thank You."

6. I listen carefully and do not interrupt.

My KCK Sales Code

7. I speak slowly, clearly, and loudly enough so people will understand me.

8. I only make promises I can keep.

9. I take an adult with me when I make face-to-face sales calls.

10. I ask God to help me find favor with everyone I meet.

The KCK Sales Code helps me make a great first impression!

With God's help, I will look great and act amazing.

The Kingdom Code